ARCHITECTURAL DESIGN

EDITORIAL OFFICES:
42 LEINSTER GARDENS, LONDON W2 3AN
TEL: 071-402 2141 FAX: 071-723 9540

HOUSE EDITOR: Maggie Toy
EDITORIAL TEAM: Nicola Hodges, Katherine MacInnes, Natasha Robertson
SENIOR DESIGNER: Andrea Bettella
DESIGN CO-ORDINATOR: Mario Bettella
DESIGN TEAM: Jacqueline Grosvenor, Jason Rigby, Owen Thomas

CONSULTANTS: Catherine Cooke, Terry Farrell, Kenneth Frampton, Charles Jencks, Heinrich Klotz, Leon Krier, Robert Maxwell, Demetri Porphyrios, Kenneth Powell, Colin Rowe, Derek Walker

SUBSCRIPTION OFFICES:
UK: VCH PUBLISHERS (UK) LTD
8 WELLINGTON COURT, WELLINGTON STREET
CAMBRIDGE CB1 1HZ UK

USA: VCH PUBLISHERS INC
303 NW 12TH AVENUE DEERFIELD BEECH, FLORIDA 33442-1788 USA

ALL OTHER COUNTRIES:
VCH VERLAGSGESELLSCHAFT MBH
BOSCHSTRASSE 12, POSTFACH 101161
69451 WEINHEIM FEDERAL REPUBLIC OF GERMANY

CONTENTS

ARCHITECTURAL DESIGN **MAGAZINE**

Maxwell **Hutchinson** Trevor Osborne • Architecture of the Imagination • The Rebuilding of Beirut • *William* **Pye** • Chicks on Form • *Michael* **Spens** Hans Hollein • Books • Reviews

War-torn Beirut, 1993

ARCHITECTURAL DESIGN **PROFILE** No 106

ORGANIC ARCHITECTURE

Sidney K **Robinson** Building as if in Eden • *Imre* **Makovecz** Anthropomorphic Architecture • *Christopher* **Day** Ensouling Buildings • *Greg* **Lynn** Multiplicitous and In-Organic Bodies • *Phil* **Hawes** Ecologically Designed Systems • *Ferenc* **Salamin** • **Arbeidsgruppen** • *John* **Lautner** • *Doug* **Garofalo** • *Terry* **Brown** • *Lester* **Korzilius** • *Arthur* **Dyson** • *Daniel* **Liebermann** • *Bart* **Prince** • *Mickey* **Muennig** • *Will* **Miller** • *Harvey* **Ferrero** • *Edward M* **Jones** • *Nari* **Gandhi** • *James T* **Hubbell**

William Pye, *Chalice*, 123 Buckingham Palace Road, London 1991

Bart Prince, Whiting Residence, Albuquerque, New Mexico

TREVOR OSBORNE

BY MAXWELL HUTCHINSON

He made and lost around £30 million. He failed to win the bid to build Richard Rogers' scheme for the extension to the National Gallery – even before the Royal carbuncle speech of 1984. He came second to Godfrey Bradman and Stuart Lipton in the Kings Cross Station competition. He has yet to realise his ambitions for a born-again St Pancras. Yet he still looks like Melvyn Bragg with a good humoured smile on his face.

Despite all this, Trevor Osborne, late impresario of Speyhawk Plc and past president of the British Property Federation, remains one of the most significant architectural patrons of the 1980s. The cheery and astoundingly ebullient Osborne has ploughed a deep furrow through the British property scene for 30 years. He has picked up fee notes from Rogers, Arup, BDP, Chapman Taylor, YRM, Rab Bennett, Fitzroy Robinson and a host of almost-rans who only qualified for the race courtesy of his patronage and faith. The story is worryingly disarming in its telling. Few could sit in a comfy chair in London's Marylebone having weathered the abuse of the world banking system, the loss of a staggering fortune and the recent failure of a long-term marriage, with such honest, transparent good humour and optimism. He reckons that the collapse of Speyhawk Plc, the company he founded and ran for a decade or more, left no architectural or construction industry creditors at its gate. So, with a clear conscience, the youthful Osborne can, with the confidence born out of a secure personal fortune, launch himself, yet again, onto the welcoming property industry.

It is difficult to tell Trevor Osborne's story: its simple, linear and predictable course belies his influence as a magnate of the 1980s property boom. It all seems so ordinary. So predictable. He rode the surf of escalating real estate values, fanned by the wind of inflation, bronzed by the sun of Thatcher monetarism and despite the wipe-out of the 90s has dusted off the sand to ride a new tide.

Underneath the suave, manicured, pinstriped facade of the man who headed up the British property industry in its finest hour, lies an impenetrable, enigmatic character whose personal skills have poured billions of honest pounds into the betterment of United Kingdom Plc's real estate portfolio. Anyone who has made and lost 30 times one million pounds in a little over ten years, celebrates his birthday at Highgrove with the Prince of Wales and can still a pour a cup of tea with a steady hand can certainly do the property hand-jive one more time.

So join with me, step back in time and ponder the genesis of a charming and good-humoured man who has pumped more dosh into British architecture than almost anyone who is prepared to stand up and be counted. Our Trev was born in Twickenham in 1943; two years before the end of what used to be called the Last War before the Falklands and the Gulf. His parents had migrated south from somewhere in the north country during the 1930s. Quite why a good, honest northern family should settle in Twickenham says more about the war and a chance, than taste or choice. After all most V-1s and doodlebugs plummeted onto the City and the West End. The sylvan, suburban glades of Twickenham seemed like a soft, safe haven.

Osborne continues to stress the suburban nature of his soul. And why not? Suburbia, lampooned as it is by the Pet Shop Boys, has become the appendix to the mainstream city. But without it much of that which is central to the city, as Osborne now understands, would lack condition and context. The suburban Osborne went to the suburban state school at Sunbury and left at the premature age of 16. 'I felt a compelling and urgent need to earn my own living. I reckoned, quite wrongly, that the best way to move forward was to begin quickly.' Whilst most around him were queuing up for the Brylcreem, draping their jackets and squeezing into 1959 drainpipes, Osborne was getting off on the houses for sale pages of the local Twickenham newspaper. 'I worked out that if I went into something, it ought to be something of high value, because my margin on it would be a large part of a large sum.' He worked out that he had to become a chartered surveyor, a member of the Royal Institution of Chartered Surveyors.

In a newly post-war Britain, institutional government at national and local level held all the cards. Osborne joined Middlesex County Council. 'They taught me how to make a cup of tea, and how to colour drawings.' Predictably he climbed the ranks from a start as the County Council's north area acquisitions junior. By good fortune his department worked at the epicentre of the British property industry in Dartmouth Street, just off St James.

By 1964, at the age of 21, he had passed all his exams and become a chartered surveyor, now South Area Estates Manager, in charge of all the Council's property in the southern area, everything from Staines to Chiswick.

With his head down he says (and I don't believe him) that he missed all the swinging 60s had to offer: 'If I'd known all that was going on I would have joined in.' Instead of hanging out in Soho, putting on the Chelsea boots and marvelling at the effect of the miniskirt on the male hormonal system, he skilfully and with Machiavellian zeal climbed the hierarchy of the Middlesex property department.

Did he have anything to do with architects? Back then in swinging 65? 'They were a rather strange bunch on the third floor with a certain amount of different style. They all wore bow ties and had long hair.' As ever was. They may have made this impact on the young Osborne, but in the early part of his career, as a small-time, suburban property developer he managed without architectural skill. As local government reorganisation spelt the end of Middlesex, he left and started a property company with Jeremy Denholm. 'I was the ideas, Jeremy was the money. I only had £100.' Neither of them seemed to have had much verbal imagination as the outfit boasted Denborne Limited as a predictable nomenclature. Denholm and Osborne worked together for eight years, splitting up in 1973 before the oil price induced collapse of the Western economy and the UK's three day week. Most of their projects seemed to be commercial schemes providing accommodation up to 10,000 square feet, for which the architects remain anonymous. 'It took me a long time to learn to use the right sort of architects.' He calls to mind Garnet Cloughly Blakemore, Edgington, Spink & Hyne, Bill Topping and the still well-known Hutchison, Locke and Monk. In a 'terribly conventional' way he married at the age of 26 and settled in a large Victorian house in east Twickenham.

When Jeremy and Trevor split in 73 the latter's 100 quid had certainly been used to good effect. He had to buy out the other half which cost him over a million pounds. Quite simply, by the age of thirty Osborne was a millionaire property developer. Despite world economic gloom and the rigor-mortis of the British property industry, Osborne started Speyhawk with its osprey logo, one of the best-known property flags of the 1980s.

From the early years Osborne can only recall half a handful of projects. The fledgling Speyhawk nested securely in the predictable, suburban, middle-class piety of west London. He converted Royal Albert House in Sheet Street and then Acre House in Windsor which he later redeveloped as part of the Edgington Spink and Hyne scheme. Five years into the new operation Osborne was joined by his friend of long standing, Derek Parkes, who acquired 20 per cent ownership. They determined to 'build first-class property investments for institutions.' Hardly a devastating mission statement it would seem but, in retrospect, an entirely new property development concept.

Speyhawk Plc was the first of what Osborne calls the 'Merchant Developers'. He claims to have invented 'forward funding'. He turned to the insurance companies, pension funds and those whose investment portfolios were in need of refreshment with the addition of good-quality, well-covenanted, secure yielding property investments. To the likes of the Post Office and electricity industry's pension funds and the insurance companies he puts it like this: 'You provide the money, we'll do everything else and we'll sell it to you when it's finished.' It may seem a blindingly obvious idea, but Osborne claims it as his own. The proof of the pudding shows he got it right.

By the early 1980s he was running up to fifteen 30,000 square foot development projects at a time – all 'forward funded'. Four years into the new company, when it was floated on the stock exchange in 1981, it was making profits of £1.5 million a year. With four times fifteen largish buildings sold down the line were there any that stood out? Were there any that were architecturally memorable? After all, this commercial through-put indicates substantial architectural patronage. Enough to make a difference. Enough to be noticed. Certainly more than most public authorities at the time and well before the

FROM ABOVE: Centre Court Wimbledon, Speyhawk Retail Plc; Harrogate Victoria Gardens; BACKGROUND: Wimbledon Bridge House

'"Welcome to the most beautiful shopping centre in Britain" and everybody cheered!'

Canon Bridge Development

Thatcher-inspired property boom of the 80s.

Speyhawk enlisted the services of at least three well-known firms: Biscoe & Stanton, Broadway & Malyan and Manning Clamp. Quite simply, when it came to the buildings, regardless of their architects or architecture Osborne 'likes them all'. Despite the extent of patronage and the financial growth of the company, it had yet to make any lasting impact on the architectural map.

The flotation was suggested and managed by Barclays de Zoete Wedd. On the day the shares hit the market Speyhawk was valued at £8.5 million. They took off and capitalised the new publicly quoted company at £11.5 million. Osborne and his family ended up owning 23 per cent of the company. By the time he rose to the top of the industry to become president of the British Property Federation in 1989 his shares were valued at around £30 million, 'which was a lot more than they were really worth'.

Speyhawk was up there with all the names; with Rosehaugh, Stanhope, Greycoat, Arlington and LET. All companies run by men of Osborne's age. Most from a similar surveying background. The 80s property brat-pack were the right age, in the right place, at the right time. The rebuilding of post-war Britain fed their entrepreneurial appetite. Little Britain had a short supply of the right land in the right places. Inflation ensured that land prices rocketed while the grass grew. Thatcher's environment henchman, Michael Heseltine, flitted about in helicopters declaring enterprise zones. The City of London changed its planning policy under the shadow of Canary Wharf: out with conservation, in with large-scale redevelopment from Broadgate downwards.

By now Osborne had learned to 'live well'. Why not, with £30 million in the company and a substantial personal fortune on top of that? He has a house in Berkshire, a flat in London, a home and a village in Cornwall and a home and a motor cruiser in Majorca. The £30 million may have disappeared when Speyhawk was finally entrusted to the receivers in 1993, but that little lot and Osborne's personal wealth remain unscathed. As we shall see, he lives to ride again.

Despite Osborne's apparent lack of architectural interest early in his career, Speyhawk grew into a substantial patron of quality architecture. BDP's Bill Jack and Richard Saxon spent £110 million of the company's money on the air rights building over the Cannon Street railway lines. An amazing technical achievement but, sad to say, pretty much typical 1980s commercial architecture with more than a little unnecessary post-modern flavouring. Some of it still lies empty.

Osborne boasts his catholic architectural taste. 'I don't fit into any camp, either the modernist or the traditionalist.' That certainly seems to sum up the philosophy (sic) of the man who dines with the Prince of Wales to discuss his Royal Highness' penchant for urban villages on the one hand whilst commissioning Richard Rogers for the most avant-garde of all the schemes for the extension to the National Gallery back in 1984 – the famous 'municipal fire station' scheme. Is this really a generous exercise of a truly broad catholic mind or a policy of the inevitable, born out of shrewd commercial pragmatism? The projects are there and speak for themselves. We judge as we find.

Osborne is most proud of two town centre redevelopments, Wimbledon by BDP and the £60 million Harrogate Victoria Gardens by David Cullearne of Manchester-based Cullearne and Phillips, which Osborne, with a twinkle in his eye, sets down like this: 'It is an absolute crib of Palladio's basilica in Vicenza, right down to a two-third scale for each bay. It has a copper domed roof and statues around the parapet. It's great! When I opened it I said: "Welcome to the most beautiful shopping centre in Britain" and everybody cheered!'

Back home at Wimbledon, Osborne commissioned Arup for a 200,000 square foot building over the railway tracks. The practice's Rab Bennett and Peter Foggo produced another reworking of the confident modernism for which the practice can be justly proud and which graces many a well-known scheme, not least the first phase of Broadgate. Rab Bennett, on his own account, built The Imperium office scheme in Reading which Osborne reckons is 'very good'.

As Osborne chats over all this lot lounging confidently in his new office, his disarmingly light-hearted manner makes it difficult to reconcile the breadth of his architectural taste. Maybe the hint lies in his choice of art? He is commissioning the surrealist Philip Bouchard to paint a series of large canvasses which depict well-known monumental buildings in a surreal landscape. First came St Pancras Station set in a romantic countryside like a dispossessed French chateau. Its architect Sir George Gilbert Scott would have loved it. The design of his floor tiles lay out the shoreline of the chateau's lake. The Gothic spires, familiarly set against the grey skies of the Euston Road, sparkle in uncharacteristic Mediterranean sunlight.

Then comes Inigo Jones' Whitehall Banqueting House represented as a Venetian Palazzo. Less surreal than the St Pancras piece but still unnerving and disorientating. Osborne does well to remind himself about St Pancras for it, along with his scheme for the Kings Cross Channel Tunnel terminal, are amongst the ones that got away.

He and contractor David McAlpine are still determined to return Scott's Hotel to its original use. Their scheme, which includes turning the station undercroft into a shopping centre, came from the unlikely drawing boards of YRM. A surreal idea at its very best. The practice which has always worn its classic modernism on its sleeve, responsible for refurbishing the country's most ridiculous neo-Gothic monument? I can only imagine that Philip Bouchard must have done the perspectives. And then Speyhawk spent around £2.5 million bidding for the Kings Cross scheme which was finally delivered into the hands of the London Regeneration Consortium headed up by Bradman and Lipton with the Foster scheme.

They spent most of that lot on the architectural work produced by the team of YRM, BDP and Chapman Taylor. 'I thought we had won it right up to the last hour.' But that was not to be.

Things started getting bad for Speyhawk back in 1989. The company was funded by no less than 46 banks. The recession was written in the tea leaves; Osborne could read them. His merchant bankers tried to find a new partner or someone to buy the company as a going concern. As the construction bandwagon rolled and office vacancies loomed, the company desperately needed more working capital. There were four interested parties. Two British companies, Dumez of France and NCC of Sweden. The Swedes were poised to make a bid when an unwitting hack spilled the beans in a piece of property gossip.

Osborne was left with the problem. He had to restructure a £100 million revolving credit facility with no less than 25 banks, all of whom had to agree as they chatted the matter over in a bewildering babble of languages. 18 months or more of negotiation finally broke down in the spring of 1993. The world's teleprinters spluttered out the message: Trevor Osborne's Speyhawk Plc had gone down.

Despite the loss of tens of millions Osborne moved quickly. He joined Hawk, the project management company which he had originally formed as Speyhawk Development Management. Most mortals would have been happy with this realignment. Not Osborne. In partnership with Pell Frishman, the co-owners of Hawk, and the construction conglomerate AMEC, he made a bid to privatise the southwest and southeast operations of the old Property Services Agency. His bid won the day.

So our young lad from Twickenham who started with a hundred pounds, made and lost £30 million, worked with some of the best-known architectural names in the business is now to be Chairman of the largest consultancy organisation in the country, employing over 3,000 staff, with a turnover of £150 million and a profit, this depressed year, of no less than £20 million.

Now separated from his wife, and his millions, Osborne seems more secure and self-assured than ever. His name is etched on the presidential medal of his industry's representative body. He may have lost a yacht or two, but judging by the hundreds of letters he received on the demise of Speyhawk, he still has friends in all the right places. More than most, of his business he proves the adage: 'It's not what you know, it's who you know.'

I remain haunted by the surrealism of his catholic architectural taste. Osborne has proved that taste in 1980s architectural patronage can be neither here nor there, but everywhere. And after all, he paid the bills. And as he himself sums up the architecture of his endeavours, 'I like them all'.

I remain haunted by the surrealism of his catholic architectural taste.

FROM ABOVE: The Imperium office scheme, Reading; Thames Valley Park

ARCHITECTURE OF THE IMAGINATION

The door, the staircase, the window, the tower and the bridge are all rich in metaphorical and psychological associations – they are places where story or drama are sharply focused and where the realms of reality and the imagination meet – these symbols flourish in everyday life. 'Architecture of the Imagination', a new series for BBC 2, explored the deeper meaning of our everyday architectural surroundings.

THE DOOR

An essential way in, as well as a means of keeping intruders out, the door has dual and contradictory roles. The doorway is a place of mystery and terror, marking a boundary between public and private space. Opening, entering, closing, slamming or locking a door are frequently made gestures that can be loaded with dramatic or psychological significance.

Ruby Gordon, from North London, has been burgled more times than she can remember. She has installed an extraordinary range of locks, grilles and alarms: 'I'm the one who feels like a prisoner.'

Nick Coogan, a six-foot three bouncer, talked of his techniques for screening customers at a London night-club. With the help of a 'sixth sense' he selects those who can be admitted to the club's inner sanctum. And in Covent Garden a Freemason explained how the Grand Master admits those on the path to initiation through the massive bronze doors of the Lodge.

Artist Ben Johnson is obsessed by doorways, and paints little else. He feels they need to be substantial, they need to make the right noise when they close. Father Benedict Ramsden, a Russian Orthodox priest, talked of the door in the church screen, which separates the altar from the rest of the church. It is, he suggested, a necessary boundary and a reminder for those who seek God

of the 'mystery of difference'.

Psychologist James Hillman suggested that the quest for openness in relationships, echoed in the development of the open-plan office, may deprive people of the personal territory which they all need and lead to tense situations.

Clips from Hitchcock's *Spellbound*, Orson Welles' *Citizen Kane*, Cocteau's *La Belle et la Bête*, Cooper and Schoedsack's *King Kong*, David Lean's *Great Expectations*, Peter Sasdy's *The Monster* and Murnau's vampire classic *Nosferatu* demonstrated the truth behind the door.

THE STAIRCASE

Whether striving towards the highest goals, or descending with terror to the abysmal depths, the staircase is a place of uncertainty and unexpected encounters, suggesting a hierarchy of good and evil, scales of achievement and the corporate ladder.

Sir Peter Holmes, the recently retired chairman of Shell, climbs to his office on the 26th floor of the Shell Tower in London every morning: 'It's a form of pain but I do it to keep fit.'

For Stuart Gray, one of British cinema's top art directors, the staircase is a secret weapon and in his latest project 'The Secret Garden', the magnificent Victorian staircase at the St Pancras Hotel plays a central dramatic role.

Architect Eva Jiricna designs highly original glass and steel staircases. Artist Deanna Petherbridge has a recurrent dream where she tries to reach her attic, but ends up in a dark, damp and bloody cellar.

Psychoanalyst Ean Begg talked of his patients dreams of staircases and the biblical story of Jacob's Ladder, the basic pattern, he believes, for many ideas about ladders of perfection. For psychologist James Hillman, the idea of a ladder or staircase leading upward to heaven is central to Western culture.

When film stars sweep down the stairs, argued Hillman, they are evoking the myth of Aphrodite or Venus, who descend from the sky to bring

beauty, grace and love to the world.

The programme included clips from Charlie Chaplin's *One AM*, George Cukor's *What Price Hollywood*, Carol Reed's *The Fallen Idol*, Boris Ingster's *film noir* classic *Stranger on the Third Floor*, Peter Hammond's *Dark Angel* and Derek Jarman's *The Tempest*.

THE WINDOW

A gap in the protective wall, the window allows in light. With its restricted view, the window focuses the imagination, framing the picture and drawing the gaze of the voyeur.

The window occupies a central place in painting. Charlotte Johnson is a painter and a seasoned voyeur. She is also aware that others watch her at her window. She paints the view from her studio, from which she can see into a hotel which rents rooms for sex by the hour.

The architect Richard MacCormac guided the programme round his chapel at Fitzwilliam College in Cambridge, with its gigantic east window overlooking a large plane tree which delicately filters the sunlight. The artist Brian Clarke remembers watching his father return from the night-shift at dawn, from a small attic window.

Psychologist James Hillman explored the way in which light has been imagined as masculine. In the paintings of the Annunciation, the Holy Spirit is often depicted as a bolt of light streaming through a window towards the Virgin Mary. And light pouring through the window is also a recurring feature of paintings in the Renaissance and Enlightenment. The lace curtains which feature in so many homes have something in common with lingerie and the erotic, suggests Hillman.

He described the 'immense pleasure in watching', ideally without being seen, and of the way in which windows, framing a particular piece of the world, stimulate the imagination. The window can be, particularly at night or during a storm, a place of terror, which no amount of

ABOVE: The massive bronze doors of the Freemasons' Lodge in Covent Garden; CENTRE: MC Escher, The Staircase; BELOW: Tarot cards depicting the tower; BACKGROUND: View of London Bridge

curtain or shutter can calm.
Michael Powell's *Peeping Tom*, Patrice Leconte's *M Hire*, Murnau's *Nosferatu* and Kieslowski's *A Short Film About Love* provided clips on this theme.

THE TOWER
Traditionally the tower is a place of incarceration but now, as in the biblical story of Babel, skyscrapers, the 20th-century's contribution to the history of towers, reach up to heaven.

The tower is also a place of retreat, the poet or philosopher's ivory tower, high above the distractions of the world. William Beckford, the 18th-century bisexual landowner and eccentric, built himself a magnificent tower just outside Bath, not only as a retreat from the world which found his eccentricities difficult to accept, but also as a place to recharge his intellectual batteries.

Historian Christopher Frayling visited the tower and reflected on Beckford's story, whilst drawing parallels with the theme of a tower in a number of cinema classics.

The writer Marina Warner warned against just seeing towers as phalluses, and spoke of the idea of the Virgin Mary as an impregnable tower, the original 'tower of ivory'.

Brian Wellington lives in a converted water-tower in Southall, which from the outside looks like a medieval fortress and stands incongruously in the midst of rows of suburban semis. 'Most people feel very secure living here,' he said.

For psychologist James Hillman, the tower is a place of seclusion, but also has a negative side as the dweller can be cut off. He suggested that the view from a tower can distort the outlook, resulting in a planner's detached overview of cities, removed from the real experience of the resident. Ironically many of the tower blocks built so proudly in the 50s and 60s are now being dynamited.

Clips featured in this programme included Shoedsack and Cooper's *King Kong*, King Vidor's *The Fountainhead* and Fritz Lang's *Metropolis*.

THE BRIDGE
The bridge makes connection, ends insularity and overcomes natural boundaries. Combining mathematical precision and beauty, it seems to defy gravity, precariously suspended over space.

Bridge-building has always been an heroic endeavour. The great civil engineers have been adventurers, testing themselves against the accidents and unpredictability of nature and experimenting with untried materials. The construction of most of the world's great bridges has been highly dangerous and has cost lives.

Richard La Trobe Batemen builds small-scale bridges, using a mixture of timber and steel cable. In sharp contrast Norman Haste is one of the most experienced bridge-builders in Britain: he is the project director on the Second Severn Crossing, being built a few miles south of the present suspension bridge. He stated that: 'We must work with nature because we will never beat it.'

Psychologist James Hillman explained that in ancient Japan only priests could build bridges, a recognition of the special qualities required. Jules Cashford, a writer on mythology, talked of the place of bridges in myths of transformation or initiation, often involving a challenge or test.

James Hillman spoke of the awe inspired by bridges and the hold they have always had on painters. Bridges bring people together and are a favourite place for lovers' trysts. They are also a place of danger, suspended between life and death.

The programme included clips from David Lean's *Bridge over the River Kwai* and *Brief Encounter*, Rob Reiner's *Stand By Me* as well as some archival documentary footage of pygmies building a bridge in the 30s and the construction of the Tyne Bridge in the late 20s.

The Window, *with (L to R) Barbara Hale as Mrs Woodry, Bobby Discoll as Tommy and Arthur Kennedy as Mr Woodry*

THE REBUILDING OF BEIRUT

The Lebanese government have employed the 2,000-strong consultancy firm Dar Al-Handasah to present a comprehensive proposal for the rebuilding of the centre of Beirut. The client for both projects is the government agency, CDR, 'Council for Development and Reconstruction'.

Dar Al-Handasah is now completing the new master plan for Beirut's city centre, an area of about 150 ha encompassing the historic core. The plan retains and restores much of the surviving fabric, severely damaged by war, and provides opportunities for archaeological excavation of important sites. The extensive shoreline landfill, originally formed from the rubble of destroyed buildings, provides space for a new city park, waterside drive and promenade, linked to the city's existing cornice, and the site for Beirut's new Financial Quarter. Dar Al-Handasah has now been commissioned to proceed to the next stage of work: detailed engineering design of the first phase infrastructures projects including roads, sewerage and storm water drainage, electrical power and telecom. Other consultants are now working on the design of the reclamation area and decontamination of the landfill to prevent further environmental pollution.

The difficulty of implementing this plan is exacerbated by financial problems. Economically the destruction of physical assets is not as significant as the erosion of the government's authority, specifically in its ability to collect taxes. Nearly 15 per cent of the population are thought to have fled in 1975 which has produced a large drop in investment capital. Funding depends on reinvestment and private external investment. The project will be realised through a novel vehicle: a real estate company – Solidère – formed by a minimum 50 per cent shareholding of existing property owners in the city centre, and new equity investors. This company will work like a British development corporation, building on existing infrastructure and refurbishing and marketing the land approved for development.

L TO R: Views of Rue Weygand before the war; and in its present condition, 1993; BACKGROUND: Rue Weygand as planned

ARCHITECTURAL DESIGN INTERVIEW WITH ANGUS GAVIN[1]

– Is there any precedent for rebuilding a city on the same site and if so how does Dar Al-Handasah's approach compare?

The real issue here is that of reconstruction of the heart of the city after its destruction by war. The centre of Beirut has in fact suffered such destruction many times in its 4,000 year history. Remains of the Phoenician, Roman and Ottoman cities are evident and will be further revealed through archaeological excavation. The archaeological dimension is a fascinating aspect of the project. The plan includes an 'archaeological park', where important discoveries are anticipated: perhaps the Roman 'School of Law' said to be sited east of the 'Etoile', the centrepiece of the French Mandate reconstruction, itself lying over the Roman Forum. For more recent inspiration we have looked at the patterns of postwar reconstruction in other, notably European cities. There are two distinct trends, and both are present here in Beirut. First, there is a strong sense of nostalgia, linked perhaps to a need to re-establish a national identity. This is most clearly expressed in the desire to faithfully recreate the fabric of the old city: Warsaw is the best example. The second trend is optimistic for the future: the old city, with its problems of land tenure, inefficient infrastructure and buildings, lack of open space and so on, has been largely swept away. We have the opportunity to re-parcel land for modern development and build a 'Brave New World', a different symbol of national reunification, looking forward to the 21st century. The 'blitzed' cities of Britain and Germany sought some of these ideals through their reconstruction.

– Some of the preliminary Master Plan images resemble the Paternoster Square pictures. Is the style and attitude classicist or is it a combination of old and new?

Much of the surviving city fabric in the historic core will be retained in the plan: heritage buildings will provide a focus and sense of 'historical memory' within new development. The planning regulations and design guidelines which we are drawing up, will encourage development sympathetic to the vernacular tradition, especially around the core and in areas in existing residential communities. Elsewhere, especially in the new 'Financial Quarter' on the waterfront reclamation area, a bold expression of contemporary architecture will be encouraged. The Client is very keen to promote quality design. The first of a series of design and urban design competitions will shortly be announced. One of these is likely to be a high-profile international competition.

– How far are you using the opportunity to create a city which is not left with an outdated 1975 structure but can be, as it were, 'computer literate'? For instance are you considering any recent theories in 21st-century communications so that, like Japan after the Second World War, Lebanon could do a 'tortoise and the hare'?

In the various economic studies and in the drawing up of floor-space budgets for the project a great deal of discussion has been centred on trends in city centre office functions – including those that run counter to

high-cost city centre location through developments in communications technologies. As a result we have progressively reduced the office context in favour of mixed use, with a strong element of inner city housing. This mixed character is considered an important aspect of the project. In terms of the technologies themselves, 'independent networks' are being considered for key utilities, in order to ensure reliability and quality of service in the city centre area. Options for state-of-the-art telecom and TV systems have been specified. One of the main objectives of the project is to re-establish Beirut's role as the financial centre of the Arab World. In order to attract international banking and financial services, sophisticated communications and information technologies are seen as essential.

– Is the development culturally sympathetic? How many of the 50-strong advisors are indigenous? Are you consulting the locals or giving them a Western solution?

Some of the preliminary Master Plan images may have given the impression that we are designing buildings. Of course this is not the case. Our main task is the urban design of the public realm, incorporating many surviving features. We believe that the new plan, significantly changed from the preliminary Master Plan of '92 which attracted a great deal of public comment, is especially sympathetic to Beirut's cultural heritage and to a sense of 'historical memory'.

There is no public inquiry system in existence here. Nevertheless there has been a very lively debate on the project in the local (and international) media and television. We have made many public presentations to professional and other interest groups. Local residents have made their views and concerns strongly felt. The Client and ourselves have responded to this open debate and I believe that the Detailed Plan, when released, will demonstrate this.

There is a small English and Belgian contingent working on the project team, including my partner, Ian Hogan. The majority are Lebanese and other Arab nationals. Many are trained in Europe or the States and have had a broad-ranging experience through the Dar 'empire'.

– Ian Thomas of Balfour Beatty felt that 'My view is that the International Bechtel/Dar Al-Handasah plan is slightly optimistic'. Which areas of your re-development plan do you think are most realistic and which optimistic?

The most realistic aspects of the plan will be the re-colonisation of the historic core and adjacent residential areas – a large-scale rehabilitation and infill programme including restoration of heritage buildings carried out by the Company, existing owners and the religious institutions. This phase will include reconstruction of the souks, almost entirely destroyed. In re-colonising the residential areas the delicate issue of dealing with and re-housing the large squatter populations will have to be addressed. I would rate as 'optimistic' the overall floor-space target of 4.4 million metres square. I think it unlikely that market demand will exist to generate such levels of development – Beirut will benefit if it does not. Also somewhat optimistic is the vision of Beirut centre as the financial capital of the Arab World. This aspect of the project – the

ABOVE: The 'etoile' centre of the new conservation area; BELOW AND OPPOSITE: Views of war-torn Beirut, 1993

development of the new Financial Quarter on the reclamation area is some 12 to 15 years away. Beirut will have to compete for this market against other cities in the Eastern Mediterranean and the Gulf. Trends in communications technologies, of course, show that such centralisation is perhaps no longer essential.
To succeed the core will have to compete against new district centres established during the war in east and west Beirut, largely as a result of the destruction of the centre. However, surveys show a preference for businesses and shops to relocate back to a renewed city centre.

– How do you see the attitude of other countries to Lebanon, for example the French connection with Oger International. How do you think international interest could be engendered without using charity which, according to the Minister of the Environment, Sir George Young, the Prime Minister and Chancellor of Lebanon do not 'expect'?

The French seem very strongly entrenched here. The British are traditionally slow at establishing a presence. I hope the Trade Delegation will have done something to reverse this. Certainly the Lebanese will welcome more international competition – for example on the major infrastructure contracts that will shortly break. The British should get on with establishing joint venture arrangements, and make sure they get on tender lists. I don't believe there is any need for foreign government grants or seed funding – these are usually tied to consultancy or supply deals. The Lebanese government sets its own priorities and agenda and does not want to be tied by such arrangements. Nevertheless, the Lebanese are entrepreneurs, and there may be scope for imaginative development funding on individual projects.

– What do you think of the Financial Times' *comparison between Switzerland and pre-war Lebanon? If it was well organised then, why can't the structures responsible for that organisation be recreated rather than introducing new solutions?*

However much like Switzerland it may have been before the war, I cannot perceive of pre-war institutions in Lebanon capable of dealing adequately with the scale of task that faces Beirut today. The city centre lies on the wartime 'Green line' and suffered much of the worst destruction during the war. A large squatter population displaced by the war occupies many of the surviving buildings. Some 30 ha of reclaimed land – originally bulldozed building rubble but, in recent years, the city's fly-tip and rubbish dump – has become a major pollution source in the eastern Mediterranean. Extreme fragmentation of land ownership and absence of capital resources to undertake the wholesale renewal of infrastructures, means that regeneration and consolidation of land for modern development cannot in my opinion take place without some new, centralising authority, with access to extensive capital resources. The concept of the real estate company – Solidère – achieves this. Although not a model likely to be feasible in a European context it will combine existing property owners as majority shareholders with new investors, who still provide capital and government's authority to build, own and maintain the new roads, public open space and infrastructure.

Interview conducted by Katherine MacInnes

References: Financial Times *9th July, 1993 Survey on Lebanon pp13-14,* Building *2nd July pp28-35*

Note

1 Angus Gavin is principal of Landseer Urban Design and is currently employed by Dar Al-Handasah to lead the Urban Design team responsible for the master planning of the reconstruction of Beirut's city centre. Previously a Development Manager with London Docklands Development Corporation he was also Principal Urban Designer for the Royal Docks. He has extensive overseas experience on large-scale urban design and development projects. Trained at Cambridge and Harvard he has also taught and lectured at UK and US architecture and planning schools.

BOOKS

RICHARD MEIER AND FRANK STELLA, Electa, Milano, 330pp, b/w ills, PB, N/A

The American artist Frank Stella has remained a prominent and innovative practitioner of abstract painting since the late 50s. Recently he has begun working on full-scale architectural projects. His collaboration with his friend the architect Richard Meier on the Palazzo delle Esposizioni presents the works of both with their magical dialogue. This exhibition is the third in an ongoing series dedicated to contemporary museum architecture which began in 1991 with the German architect Josef Paul Kleihues' museum designs followed by Constantino Dardi 1992. This publication which accompanies the exhibition, discusses Richard Meier's designs for the new Getty Center in Los Angeles, the Barcelona Museum of Contemporary Art and several other museum buildings. A selection of Frank Stella's paintings from the 1960s and 70s, wall relief pieces from the 1980s Moby Dick series and a recent monumental sculpture are discussed in the text. The catalogue includes extensive biographies and its generous use of images provides a clear analysis of their philosophy.

SPLENDOURS OF THE BOSPHORUS, Houses and Palaces of Istanbul by Chris Hellier and Francesco Venturi, Tauris Parke, 1993, 230pp, colour ills, HB £34

Istanbul is a city poised on the threshold of two continents, with the Bosphorus strait flowing through its centre separating European and Asian Turkey. This is one of the world's most beautiful and romantic waterways, navigated by Jason and the Argonauts and eulogised by poets and writers as varied as Lord Byron, Lamartine and Lady Mary Wortley Montagu. On the shores of the Bosphorus, Eastern and Western cultures meet – their eclectic and dynamic mix is supremely evident in the houses and palaces built on the waterfront by generations of Ottoman families.

The Bosphorus embraces a wealth of magnificent architecture: the 15th-century Topkapi Palace which still dominates the skyline of Istanbul; the unique red, yellow, pink and green facades of wooden mansions known as 'yalis', built during the prosperous 'Tulip Period' of the 18th century; the increasingly cosmopolitan buildings of the early 19th-century; and the Graeco-Roman styles re-introduced by later Sultans.

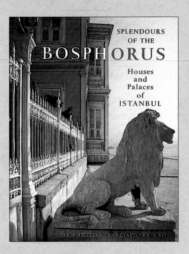

GERTRUDE JEKYLL, 1843-1932, A Celebration, The Museum of Garden History, 58pp, b/w ills, PB N/A

One of the most engaging features of this catologue are the sketches by Lutyens of the matronly figure of Gertrude Jekyll as an angel flying across the page, wand in hand. His tongue in cheek 'I make obeisance', which shows him prostrate in front of Jekyll, shows that she was not his gardener but an 'artiste' in her own right. They show a great friendship which was the basis for a collaboration between architect and landscape/garden designer for many years. This imbues their projects with a humanity that was almost unique to the Arts & Crafts movement – the formalism of the 'embroidered' gardens of the middle ages and Capability Brown's 'shaven lawns' were devoid of this intention. Jekyll was one of the few women of her time to be considered the professional equal of a man.

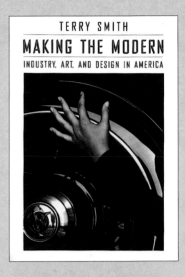

MAKING THE MODERN Industry, Art and Design in America by Terry Smith, University of Chicago Press, 1993, 510pp b/w ills, HB N/A

Terry Smith chronicles the modernist revolution in American art and design – from its origins in the new industrial culture of the 20th century to its powerful and transforming effects on the way Americans came to see themselves and their world. From Ford Motor's first assembly line in 1913 to the New York World's Fair in 1939, Smith traces the distinctive visual imagery that evolved as the core of American modernity in the first half of the 20th century. Through visual images such as Albert Kahn's plant designs, Charles Sheeler's industrial landscapes, Margaret Bourke While's photographs, Diego Rivera's Detroit murals, the design of *Fortune* magazine and advertising, the FSA historical project allows a historical interpretation. From the role of visualisation in the invention of the assembly line, to office and building design, to the corporate and lifestyle images that filled new magazines such as *Life* and *Fortune*, he traces the extent to which the second wave of industrialisation engaged the visual arts to project a new iconology of progress.

THE SEVEN AGES OF FRANK LLOYD WRIGHT by Donald W Hoppen, Capra Press, Santa Barbara, 1993, b/w ills, PB N/A

This biography of the life and work of Frank Lloyd Wright by a former apprentice and Taliesin fellow is the first book to explain and illustrate the evolution and meaning of Wright's architecture. During the course of his research, Hoppen

BOOKS RECEIVED:

BERLIN, The Politics of Order 1737-1989 *by Alan Balfour, Rizzoli, New York, 267pp, b/w ills, HB £27.50*

MONUMENTS & NICHE, The Architecture of the New City *by Carsten Juel-Christiansen, Rhodos, Copenhagen, 82pp, b/w and colour ills, HB N/A*

THE WILD CARD OF DESIGN, A perspective on architecture in a project management environment *by Kenneth Allinson, Butterworth Heinemann, Oxford, 436pp b/w ills, HB £35*

RUSSIAN HOUSING IN THE MODERN AGE, Design and Social History, *Cambridge University Press, a Woodrow Wilson Centre Series edited by William Craft Brumfield Blair A. Ruble, 322pp, b/w ills, N/A*

A TASTE OF HISTORY, 10,000 YEARS OF FOOD IN BRITAIN, *English Heritage in association with British Museum Press, 351pp, b/w ills, PB £14.95*

THE LANDMARKS OF NEW YORK *by Barbaralee Diamonstein, Abrams, 480pp, b/w and colour ills, HB £40*

CHICAGO ARCHITECTURE AND DESIGN *by George A Larson and Jay Pridmore, Abrams, 256pp, b/w and colour ills, HB £40*

COUNTRY HOUSES OF ENGLAND *by Geoffrey Tyack and Stephen Brindle, Blue Guide Series, A&C Black, 608pp, b/w ills, maps and plans, PB £15.99*

MORE THAN THE SUM OF OUR BODY PARTS *by CARY, Chicks in Architecture Refuse to Yield (To Atavistic Thinking in Design and Society), 55pp, b/w and colour ills, PB N/A*

ARATJARA, Art of the First Australians *edited by Bernard Lüthi, DuMont Buchverlag Köhn, 379pp, PB £19.95*

admitted to being '. . . surprised by Wright's lack of bitterness after a turbulent lifetime that included more than a normal share of tragedy. But like the phoenix, each disaster would lead to yet another metamorphosis of his work.' When Hoppen first arrived at Taliesin East he found Wright directing his apprentices in an ambitious tree-planting scheme to screen the neighbouring houses, many of which he had designed when he was young and could no longer tolerate. If they were beyond help he tried to buy them, whereupon the Fellowship would throw a party and burn them to the ground.

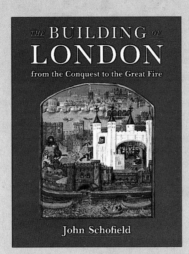

THE BUILDING OF LONDON From the Conquest to the Great Fire by John Schofield, British Museums Press in association with The Museum of London, 190pp, b/w ills, PB 14.95
What did the medieval and Tudor city of London look like? And how did it grow from its Roman and Saxon origins to a great European metropolis? For the first time in paperback the evidence is brought together to present a detailed and absorbing picture of the evolution of the nation's capital up to the Great Fire. Although the old city was virtually destroyed, a few medieval buildings, such as the Guildhall, still remain. More evidence survives in legal documents, maps and plans, and antiquarian drawings. Most exciting of all are the new discoveries of urban archaeology. This survey takes us from London's early days as a Roman provincial capital up to the teeming city, packed with old timber-framed buildings, which was a natural prey to the disastrous fire that struck in 1666.

INTERNATIONAL COMPETITION FOR URBAN DESIGN IDEAS 1993, Parliament District at the Spreebogen Capital, Berlin, Bauwelt, 200pp, b/w ills, PB N/A
The Spreebogen Competition for Germany's government district and political centre in Berlin was the largest urban design competition ever to be held. A total of 1,912 architects requested the competition brief, and 835 entries from 488 countries were submitted – among them 156 from Germany, 121 from Italy, 106 from France and 92 from the USA. On 18th February 1993 the international jury of architects and political representatives decided in favour of the submissions by the Berlin architect Axel Schultes.

This book is the complete documentation of all 835 entries, based on the architects' original material. Particular attention is given to Axel Schultes' winning entry, as well as to the other award-winning submissions and honourable mentions. All other entries are presented in typological order, which renders them highly assessable for analysis. The index contains the comprehensive name list of all contributing architectural practices – thus this documentation becomes a general study on the state of the art of urban planning today as well as an international work of reference.

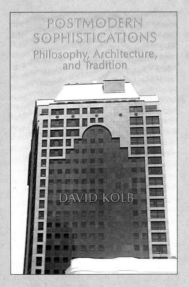

POSTMODERN SOPHIST-ICATIONS, Philosophy, Architecture and Tradition by David Kolb, The University of Chicago Press, Chicago, 216pp, b/w ills, PB £11.25
'The word postmodern now slips easily off the tongue, along with post-industrial, post-colonial, post-patriarchal, and the like. While it may become too vague, there are important issues to be considered in its vicinity. So much of our thinking about ourselves revolves around the division between traditional and modern: the old secure life versus the new rootless life where traditional values are attacked (or traditional restrictions finally broken).' Kolb discusses post modern architectural styles and theories within the context of philosophical ideas about modernism and postmodernism. He focuses on what it means to dwell in a world and with a history and to act from or against a tradition.

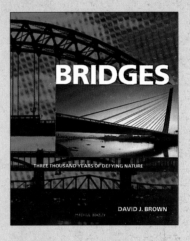

BRIDGE DESIGN The Royal Fine Art Commission Seminar, HMSO publications, 41pp, colour ills, PB £13.50
Few man-made structures combine the technical with the aesthetic in such an evocative way as is achieved through the bridge. The long history of bridges is illustrated throughout this book: pre-2000 BC, primitive suspension bridge techniques in China and India. Projects by famous engineers such as Thomas Telford, Robert Stephenson, John Roebling, Gustave Eiffel and Santiago Calatrava are presented with good colour images accompanied by a clear informative text. Brown analyses the history of the of the most beautiful and popular tourists sights in Europe: the Karlsbrüke in Prague; the Rialto in Venice – he explains how each bridge was constructed using diagrams and cross sections. The concept of bridging is discussed through references from the Iron Bridges of the Industrial Revolution to the Danish, Great Belt Link and proposals for the future.

REVIEWS

IS STARCK A DESIGNER?

'Picasso of the 90s' – brilliant designer or shock man? Sir Terence Conran says, 'I always use his lemon squeezer even though I know I'll be spattered with juice.' Surely one of the factors to determine a good designer is the functionalism of his products? How can this designer/pop star get away with such foibles? What could be more practical than environmental responsibility? The 'Louis 20' recyclable chair allows for the separation of the recyclable materials aluminium and plastic. In order for the basic materials not to be mixed with additives, a surface finish was avoided and glue was replaced with screw joints.

Design Museum, London 17 June – 3 October 1993

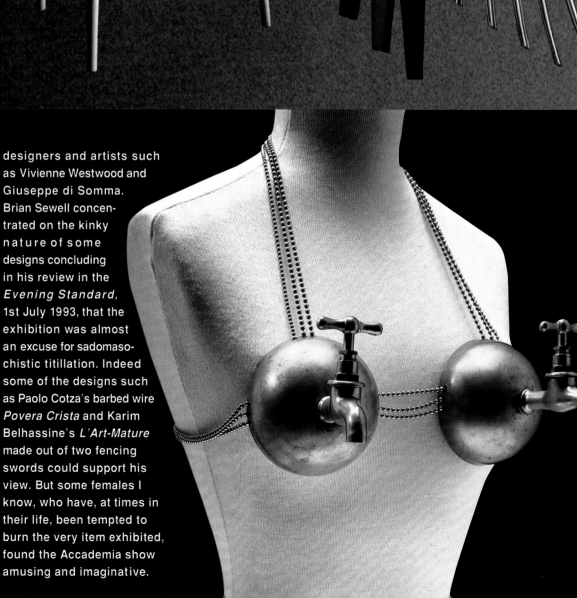

'HURRAH FOR THE BRA'

The exhibition held at the Accademia Italiana celebrates the bra as an art form. It surveys a selection of over 2, 000 bras belonging to the Florentine fashion guru Samuele Mazza, created by contemporary Italian artists and designers. The exhibition is divided into three sections: the first examines the history of the bra and examples include a war time bullet-proof bra and the bra worn in Franco Zeffirelli's 1963 production of *Aida* at La Scala; the second focuses on painted bras by Italian artists, one by Samuele Mazza himself. The final section is dedicated to designer bras, which include the most weird and innovative bras created by international designers and artists such as Vivienne Westwood and Giuseppe di Somma. Brian Sewell concentrated on the kinky nature of some designs concluding in his review in the *Evening Standard,* 1st July 1993, that the exhibition was almost an excuse for sadomasochistic titillation. Indeed some of the designs such as Paolo Cotza's barbed wire *Povera Crista* and Karim Belhassine's *L'Art-Mature* made out of two fencing swords could support his view. But some females I know, who have, at times in their life, been tempted to burn the very item exhibited, found the Accademia show amusing and imaginative.

TINY TEMPLE OF CONVENIENCE

*Down gleaming walls of porc'lain flows the sluice
That out of sight decants the kidney juice
Thus pleasuring those gents for miles around Who, crying for relief, once piped the sound
Of wind in alley-ways. All hail this news*

The 'best lavatory in the world' has been erected in Westbourne Grove, W2. It has been paid for by local residents who rejected the mediocre design proposed by their local authority, calling it an insult to their neighbourhood, in favour of a design by Piers Gough of CZWG. The building is constructed on a traffic island on the Notting Hill carnival route. The triangular shape rises with a cantilevered glazed fan-roof and a florist's kiosk at one end. The walls are clad in turquoise glazed bricks. Dancing figures are etched on the silver doors to catch and reflect the light of the sun. It has been hailed as a triumph for the avant-garde.

ARCHETYPE MAGAZINE

Perhaps the most attractive feature of *Archetype* is that publicising student work will be its priority – its raison d'être even. As a 'voice for students' Sacha Cole, RIBA student representative for 1993-94, claims that *Archetype* will improve communications between architectural students and the RIBA. He is confident in his goal, having already received over 3,000 student subscriptions – 'more student subscriptions than any existing publication can boast!' With two years of planning behind it, *Archetype*'s business plan presents a thoroughly professional and convincing projection of its viability and market. The preview was sent out to potential sponsors, advertisers and to 4,000 students on September 27th this year.

Cole claims that there are 'no national architectural magazines catering specifically for student needs, they are spread throughout the spectrum of magazines. We want to make them physically more accessible by putting them all in one place.'

Financially we are reversing the trend with a free controlled circulation to students – because *Archetype* is free, we are not preventing students from being able to afford to subscribe to other magazines.'

Archetype will be 'user friendly' with most articles supported by a thoroughly researched fact file. Jargon is explained, a definition of *isms* provided – a priori knowledge is not always assumed. Cole explains, 'if, for example, we are featuring Louis Kahn, we would not just talk about one of his projects but give a brief career and project history – simple back-up information and source referencing to encourage further research.' A 'walk-about' feature aimed at discouraging armchair magazine architecture suggests routes around various cities providing an architectural analysis of significant buildings.

The magazine is requested, each issue is going out individually addressed. Its anticipated initial circulation will be 5,000 rising to 15,000 by the end of the first year. Cole reminds his target audience that they would do well to remember that 'students will become the architects of the future'.

Contact: Sasha Cole, Archetype Office – tel: 071 607 4558

REVIEWS

PRINCE OF WALES'S INSTITUTE OF ARCHITECTURE
FOUNDATION COURSE END OF YEAR SHOW

Rich in the variety of exhibits shown, it reveals the specific skills of each student from art through craft to architecture. As Claudia Vogelsang, herself a student, observes, 'the course profited from the range of skills amongst students' – each brought their own interests and qualifications to bear giving the exhibition an impression of a collection of first attempts studded with polished gems. Although all the students are encouraged to experiment with the spectrum of architectural and artistic methods, the fantastic water-

colours of 33-year-old Ivan Kniazev, previously an architect in St Petersburg, are extraordinarily eloquent, combining precision with his remarkable imagination. The intricate wooden architectural models of Ralph Perry Robinson, the 28 year old builder and furniture maker, present a similarly detailed but contrastingly three-dimensional exhibit while the simple harmony of the 'Green Room' betrays Claudia Vogelsang's previous training in landscape architecture.

This was no dress rehearsal, the 3D geometric forms stalking the garden of Gloucester Gate are merely the beginnings of evidence to suggest that these students were encouraged to

realise the effects of their training within the year.

28 renaissance men and women will graduate from the Institute this year, but how many of them are going to pursue a career in architecture after being tempted by the delights of every other method of artistic expression under the stars? The answer is the majority. There are five exceptions to the rule and five who hope to join the Institute's graduate course – the remaining eighteen are moving on to other architectural courses. Their reaction will be an interesting indication of how well the Prince's Institute prepares its students for a life in the 'real world' of architecture.

FOSTER ASSOCIATES
TORRE DE COLLSEROLA, BARCELONA

In May 1988 Sir Norman Foster and Partners won a competition for a 'monumental technological element' as the City of Barcelona described it – the Torre de Collserola, designed by Ove Arup and Partners and built by the Spanish contractors Cubiertas y MZOV with Spanish engineer Julio Martinez Calzon, was officially inaugurated on 27 June 1992.

With its public viewing gallery and glass lift stands, the Torre de Collserola stands 288 metres tall on the ridge of Collserola, dominating the city. A conventional tower of this height would need a shaft at least 25 metres in diameter. The

Torre de Collserola has a 4.5 metre diameter hollow slip-formed reinforced concrete main shaft which reduces to a mere 300mm to hold a radio mast which telescopes from 2.7-0.7 metres. The structure is held to the mountainside by three pairs of guys, made from pre-tensioned high-strength steel which means that the tower is stable under extreme wind conditions.

13 main floors (which could contain 900 people) are surrounded by a perimeter of open stainless steel grilles and suspended from the shaft by three primary vertical steel trusses. The upper guys are made from Aramid fibre cable which does not conduct electricity so makes unrestricted transmission and reception of signals possible.

'THE HISTORY OF ARCHITECTURAL GLASS AND BUILDING TECHNOLOGY' – PROFESSOR DAVID BUTTON

The idea of glass as a beautiful material in its own right found a continuing embodiment in the architecture of Gropius, Mies van der Rohe and Le Corbusier.
'It stands for the illumination of the dark places of vernacular superstition by the pure light of rationality. World-wide, it has become the symbolic material of clarity, literal and phenomenal.'

Glass has its own material developments which have, and will bring, new aesthetic qualities to architecture.

The building structure is no longer of primary architectural importance; of equal design consideration and equal financial investment, are the heating, lighting and air conditioning services. The age old load-bearing wall of brick and stone gave relatively high thermal insulation and thermal capacity with low solar admission. Up to 1900 the multi-cellular building was, by modern standards, still heavyweight and able to absorb much of the daily climatic fluctuations; but from this time onwards, building structures become increasingly lighter and building fabric increasingly permeable to heat transfer, producing potentially a more capricious internal environment. The metabolic balance of the modern building greatly relies on its own internal services. Building structure has changed from a load-bearing facade to an internal skeletal form with changing implications for the building services.

In 1904 the separate developments in air conditioning and architecture came together in Frank Lloyd Wright's Larkin Building, Buffalo, USA, which he claimed as the first air conditioned building. Since glass has become a major part of that skin it has new responsibilities in the form of new performance requirements. For example, the need for solar attenuation, because of the solar loading from the glass skin and the low thermal mass of lightweight skeletal structures, became an important issue in the thermal behaviour of buildings. During the 1920s the development of air conditioning for multi-cellular buildings by Carrier and others to some extent obscured these solar over-heating problems in the United States. With the sophistication of the building services, and demand for increased occupant comfort glass, products were developed with coatings for solar energy attenuation, as was multiple glazing for thermal insulation.

The window has become a selective filter of solar energy and, with the advent of low emissivity coatings, a key element in passive solar energy design in energy efficient buildings with reduced CO_2 emission. The modern liberated window had dissolved to become part of a transparent skin potentially admitting an abundant flow of daylight to every corner of the building. Modern architects seemed to have forgotten the age-old preoccupation with model-ling the interior with natural light, except perhaps for Le Corbusier, Frank Lloyd Wright and Aalto, for whom it remained a vital architectural tool. Thomas Edison emerged at the end of the 19th century as the father of electric lighting. With the growth in electrical power and distribution industries, the designer was suddenly provided with new, fascinating means of illumination. From now on the window had to be considered in relation to artificial illumination.

It is no good having a sophisticated mechanical services system for a building and a poor skin performance. It is only even partially effective to have a sophisticated mechanical services installation and high quality fixed performance skin. A time responsive, variable quality skin system is the only logical answer to this problem. A building becomes a chameleon which adapts.

In the last few years there has been much research on variable transmission glass, directed initially to the automotive industry. New technologies in photochromic, thermochromic and electrochromic devices have excited the interest of researchers; their study of variable transmission is driven by a desire for energy saving and improved levels of comfort. Variable transmission facades in the future could be controlled personally or by climatic sensors linked to the central services control. This technology will find its place in windows, translucent walls and internal screens; it will also have a dynamic effect on the appearance of the interior and exterior of buildings.

ABOVE: Mies van der Rohe, Glass Skyscraper model 1922 ; BELOW: Willis Polk, Hallidee Building, San Francisco 1918; BACKGROUND: James Carpenter, Los Angeles Pilkington Planar Project with dichroic coating 1992.
Extract from a lecture from the 12th Annual Seminar of the Construction History Society, 11 August 1993, Science Museum, London

WILLIAM PYE

'IF I WERE CALLED IN TO CONSTRUCT A RELIGION I SHOULD MAKE USE OF WATER.'

Water *by Philip Larkin*

The beguiling qualities of water appeal to our most basic instincts. Water is a seductive element and if one considers the mass appeal of the Trevi fountain or the fountains in the Piazza Navona (these are after all a synthesis of sculpture and water), one can appreciate that it is the water which has helped the sculptures to become so universally accessible. It is true that most people are drawn to fountains, waterfalls and water features in a way that is often denied to public sculpture.

It is those repeating yet infinitely complex and ever-changing patterns of water which are so mesmeric and compulsive, something akin to the hypnotic effect of staring into a flickering fire, each lick of flame repeating itself, yet different every time. *William Pye, 1993*

Formed in 1990 the William Pye Partnership combines sculpture studios with a professional architectural practice. His work presents another angle on organic architecture as discussed in the main body of this magazine. His commissions involve incorporating the three disciplines of sculpture, architecture and landscaping by internalising features of the external environment to elicit the same feeling of calm and wellbeing experienced when watching water in streams and pools outside.

Arethusa, commission for the foyer of Unicorn House, Euston Road, London in 1989-90, seems to represent all the elements by incorporating a pool which is contoured at different levels into terraces suggesting a shallow landscape set against the backdrop of a water wall – a sheer curtain of water cascading down a glass wall

ABOVE AND BACKGROUND: Water wall and portico, British Pavilion, Expo 92, Seville; BELOW: Slipstream Gatwick North Terminal

which extends across the entire width of the foyer. The descending roll-wave patterns on the glass are echoed by their reflections in the pool rising to meet them. Stairs cantilevered over the water give access to the first floor whilst enabling one to experience the water effects at close quarters. The most fascinating quasi-architectural feature is the narrow slot which separates the marble front and the water which are both set at the same level producing a trompe d'oeil effect, questioning where the architecture ends and the sculpture begins.

The idea for the sculptures originated in a natural phenomenon I had observed in nature . . . One typically rainy day as I was walking along a descending road I became aware that the thin film of rainwater running over the road surface was collecting into surprisingly regular formation. These were moving down hill at an easy walking pace, with a gap of approximately 18 inches between each. The effect was curiously beautiful, but so slight as to be easily missed and to go unnoticed. I was particularly fascinated by the mesmeric effect of these waves with their endlessly repeating, yet infinitely complex and ever changing patterns. The effects of this discovery are incorporated in his best known work, *Slipstream*, in Gatwick North Terminal, commissioned in 1986-88. Large asymmetrical cones of

mirror polished stainless steel exploit the effect of 'lamina flow' in which a film of falling water is pulled by surface tension into rhythmical wave patterns – inspired by the patterns he had observed.

Epidavros, a combination of the three disciplines, was achieved by creating a paved courtyard as a setting for this sculpture. Epidavros is a renowned Greek theatre in the Peloponnese where tiers of stone seating are built into a hillside – the apotheosis of hard landscaping, acknowledging the terrain whilst imposing a human order upon it, an historic example of the combination of sculpture and landscape architecture. The bronze fan-shaped weir of *Epidavros* is reminiscent of the fan-shaped theatre, with the water evoking the stage.

An example of Pye's architectural response to space is the *Chalice* commissioned by Grey Coat London Estates for 123 Buckingham Palace Road in 1990-91. To avoid the cliched phallic water spout which the shape of this vertical space seemed to suggest, inspired by the Sultan Hassan mosque in Cairo, Pye decided to hang the sculpture from a ring suspended up among the roof trusses of the cupola using 120 stainless steel cables. As the light catches these cables, one perceives a vast ethereal cylinder within the overall space articulated by the cables. Jets rise and fall within the massive steel bowl, over six metres in diameter, hovering three metres above the floor

FROM ABOVE: View and detail of Arethusa, Unicorn House, Euston Road, London

Water cascades down to ground level from an aperture in the bottom of the bowl where it flows over a green bronze apron.

The Waterwall for the British pavilion, Seville, Spain, 1990-92, was significant in the fact that the Pye Grimshaw partnership demonstrated the effectiveness of the complete integration of sculpture and architecture. Colin Amery of the *Financial Times* observed that:

. . . the idea behind the British pavilion was to bring the sound and presence of moving water to the dry, hot island of La Cartuja . . . It would have been easy to design another fountain or a leafy courtyard, but Grimshaw decided to make the whole front of the pavilion a wall of moving water.

The Portico comprises two curtains of water created by arcs sculpted in mirror-polished stainless steel, marking the narrow entrance bridge which passes over a moat. Each arc is cantilevered from a vertical pole using elegantly tensioned cables to minimise the structure's volume. The east wall is made of panes of glass suspended from stainless steel brackets infront of which there is a continuous waterfall.

Epidavros *Dolby Laboratories, Wooton Bassett, Wiltshire opened 23 April, 1993*

CHICKS ON FORM

The number of women architects is rising rapidly', according to the recent report of the Women Architects Committee of the RIBA. The statistics they use to substantiate this premise are that women now represent 9 per cent of the profession as a whole and 27 per cent of new entrants to architecture courses. It is exactly this discrepancy between the number of female architectural students and the number of professionals that betrays the root of the problem. Where do the remaining 18 per cent of qualified female architects go?

CARY (Chicks in Architecture Refuse to Yield) the Chicago based organisation, has recently exhibited a piece called 'More than the Sum of our Body Parts' which was accompanied by text comparing the role of women in Law, Medicine and Architecture entitled 'Three Pros in a Boat'. Its research suggests parallels in the American system where, although 29.2 per cent of architectural students are female, they constitute only 5.6 per cent of the AIA membership.

The question of women in architecture is frequently referred to but seldom properly addressed. The recent report prepared by the Women Architects Committee of the RIBA was put to the Council of the RIBA in a meeting on the 14th July. While the RIBA did not oppose the recommendations, they gave no indication of timing or funding. Page 15 of the survey concludes with an unhelpfully vague list of the advantages of being a woman architect as indicated through an analysis of the data collected – more able to listen to and empathise with clients and other professionals; better skills than men in certain areas; a high profile which is a positive advantage and the possibility of flexible working. This typically grey event has not caused even a ripple in the media, trade or otherwise.

Architect Carol Carndall of CARY notes that the AIA has its first woman president, Susan Maxman, but says that Ms Maxman is more interested in the environment than in the condition of women in architecture. President Maxman, from Baltimore, says she can do more for women architects by being a good architect than by pursuing women's issues.

Denise Scott Brown and her husband Robert Venturi form the well known practice Venturi Scott Brown whose best known work in Britain is the extension to the National Gallery. 'Public Space and Public Work', the recent BBC Open University programme, suggests that it is her husband's name that is publicly associated with the building – her response: 'I think it's very difficult for women still in architecture and maybe even more in America than in Europe. And I've pondered a long while as to why this is so, but the more the building is caught up with symbolism, the more the need is to make an architectural star and the star needs to be a man. The architectural prima donnas are all male.'

The BBC programme suggests that Foster Associates – Norman and Wendy Foster – was a good example of a wife's reputation being subsumed under her husband's name. In an article written by Wendy Foster when the Sainsbury Centre at the University of East Anglia was first built, she described the Centre as their building, what they have done, their goals. In current architectural publications, her name is no longer associated with it.

Odile Decq and Beniot Cornette provide a useful counter-argument for the tendency to attribute work to the male in a partnership. Decq's striking appearance produces a lasting impression and although the partnership is well established they have had to remind the media to credit both. The project range of this partnership defies gender categorisation – from crêches, for Hospital Bichat and later Beclere in Paris in the early 1980s to Law Courts in Avesnes sur Helpe, Paris and the Regional Headquarters for Apple, Nantes.

The problem of attribution has many permutations. Although Belgium would seem to be a more liberated country than either Itsuko Hasegawa's Japan or Zaha Hadid's Iran, it has not all been plain sailing for the architect Jose van Hee. In a preface to her architectural autobiography, Hilde Peleman draws an subtle analogy between a point in van Hee's career and the Le Corbusier/Eileen Gray case. For many years Eileen Gray's house E1027, on the French Riviera, was wrongly attributed to Corbusier. Corbusier, a great admirer of the building, never took the trouble to rectify this error.

Peter Cook and Christine Hawley represent a partnership which actively seek equal recognition. Cook, of Archigram fame, is aware that the wide exposure given to his early theories should not eclipse the importance of Hawley's projects such as The Shadow House for the partnership's oeuvre. Hani Rashid and Lise Anne Couture form Studio Asymptote, a younger partnership on the other side of the Atlantic. After the first hour of the 'Theory and Experimentation' symposium held at the Royal Academy in 1992, the co-chairman Robert Maxwell asked to hear 'a woman's voice'. Hani Rashid had given the formal address while Lise Anne Couture was forced to make three attempts to be heard. Even Dagmar Richter, who had been asked to prepare a slide presentation, encountered similar difficulties.

Despite the male-dominated tendencies of Japanese society, Itsuko Hasegawa has challenged the present tendency to analyse in a formalist way. Taki Koji dismisses those critics who attribute her delicate designs to feminine decorative tendencies arguing that 'her projects have the appearance of an aspect of society made comprehensible in the form of architecture' suggesting, as the RIBA report concludes, that women show a greater empathy with the 'client'. The Shiranui Psychiatric Hospital and Stress Care Centre in Ohmuta is a good example of Hasegawa's dialogue-based programme. She and the client spent three years discussing the relationship between architecture and medical care to ensure a holistic architectural response. This experimental therapeutic space was achieved through the use of light reflected from the sea which also provides the comfort of the natural rhythm of the tides. Similarly, for the Shonandai Cultural Centre, Hasegawa involved the local residents allowing close communication between the design team and the community.

Zaha Hadid comes from an even more male dominated society – Iran. Projects such as Folly 3 in Osaka; Moonsoon Restaurant in Sapporo; the Vitra Fire Station in Weil am Rhein and Media Park, Zollhof have made her one of the best respected female architects today. Her designs prove that there is no particular style for women. Traditionally it is assumed that men design obelisks while women create cosy enveloping womb-like spaces; men go from macro to micro and women from micro to macro. The argument arises from the fact that men and women have different bodies and that if the body is the way we experience the world then subjective interpretation leads to the above forms. For the same reason, unlike 'male architecture', forms designed by women will be 'receiving', using a more compact design with less external features.

Zaha Hadid's work is confident and dynamic, frequently using vertical emphasis – for example, two vertically extruded planes signal Folly 3 to approaching visitors who move along the ground or through the air by means of monorail. The Moonsoon Restaurant as an interior contradicts its exterior enclosure challenging the tendency to internalise often attributed to female designers. The dynamic forms used by Hadid serve to present the argument for a 'particular style for women' as null and void.

The work mentioned thus far, pre-empts the question posed in *Public Works and Public Space* – 'Do women consume architecture differently and if so should architects, particularly women architects, design differently to take these different needs into account?' The argument follows a predictable line: more likely to be looking after someone/ doing house work therefore less mobile; less likely to have access to a car because of money issue; more likely to be using social services, shops etc. Should public transport systems/buildings, waiting rooms, tubes, shops and lavatories be designed by women, their most frequent users, who understand the awkwardness of accommodating children? The women architects mentioned above are testimony to the fact that, even if women are more empathetic to 'domestic' issues, they are equal to men in their design of ambitious large-scale projects of international significance making a convincing case for swift implementation of the recommendations of the Women Architects Committee to ensure that they are practically able to continue this important work.

Sheila Miller, a member of the Steering Committee, pointed out that some of the recommendations require governmental intervention, for example: 'Adopt a policy in favour of requesting tax relief for child-care expenses for women architects and requesting more widespread facilities for after-school and holiday care.' A recommendation to prepare a 'Good Practice Guide' providing guidelines for part and flexi-time work, is planned for stage 3 of the Strategic Study programme which means that it cannot become applicable until next year. Miller claims that it is difficult to answer the question of funding since they did not have time to go through resources before presenting the report and different recommendations involve specific departments. For example, the suggestion that 'suitable schemes of professional indemnity insurance and CPD should be available to architects who work part-time or take a career break' applies specifically to the education department.

In his article, 'Rising stars for the year 2000', the *Sunday Telegraph*'s architectural correspondent Kenneth Powell asked who will replace Norman Foster, Richard Rogers and James Stirling as the Big Three architects of the 21st century. He chose Will Alsop, Future Systems (the Jan Kaplicky and Amanda Levete partnership) and Zaha Hadid. Therefore, if we are to believe Powell's prediction, there will be two women out of four represented in the world of up and coming famous architects. This is an extraordinary ratio, and one which is not yet numerically reflected in the practice.
By Katherine MacInnes

ABOVE: Future Systems, Green Building; BELOW: Dagmar Richter, sculpture for Theory and Experimentation Exhibition, London, 1992; BACKGROUND: Itsuko Hasegawa, Oshima Machi Picture Book Museum, 1992

HANS HOLLEIN

Michael Spens

A new project completed by Hans Hollein is invariably an architectural event and the official, celebratory opening of the new complex of offices and apartments for the major Austrian insurance and financial services company Erste Allgemeine Generali at Bregenz in Western Austria was no exception this June.

The isometric shows the essential strengths this new assemblage of urbane buildings offers to Bregenz, a long-established frontier town close to the Swiss border and Lake Constanz. The spaces at ground level, between the buildings and also aligned to colonnades beneath each of the three buildings, were considered by Hollein to be as important as the internal space provided. In both cases the results have been exemplary. First impressions, too, are of a high quality, high-cost and stylish group of buildings replete with established Hollein visual elements, and this is particularly evident in the polished stonework and marble finishes: no less so in the superb disposition of the lighting systems, both in the offices and in the residential apartments which fill two of the buildings. Circulation spaces and lobbies reveal such Hollein skills as cannot be replicated, and alert the mind for finishes of special distinction. Nonetheless, this project was finished within budgets set in original competition. This efficiency in site and project management and the ability to produce quality at economically acceptable levels is a characteristic of the Hollein office, of which the Mönchengladbach city art gallery (1984) has been an example.

The largest of the three distinct buildings houses the offices of the group, while the remaining two buildings contain apartments. Views from the top (conference room level) of the EA Generali offices, or indeed from the superb penthouses at the uppermost level of the central, curved residential block are magnificent, over the outskirts of Bregenz, towards the Alps.

The Bregenz group of buildings was celebrated with due aplomb in traditional Austrian ways at the opening; and yet it is essentially a very low-key, workaday project. It is surely an index of true professionalism that it can be so readily accomplished, and seem so inherently normal, as a new arrival in Bregenz, while yet proving so superlative in terms of finished design. While the Hollein Atelier has accomplished much-publicised masterpieces in major city locations, there is surely no clearer sign of the office's professional dedication than can be so enjoyably made manifest in this excellent everyday scheme.

EA Generali, the clients, are to be congratulated too for their intelligent realisation of the importance of quality at every level of operation.

ORGANIC ARCHITECTURE

ARBEIDSGRUPPEN, WALDORF SCHOOL, STAVANGER, NORWAY

Architectural Design

ORGANIC ARCHITECTURE

ABOVE: ARTHUR DYSON, JAKSHA RESIDENCE, MADERA COUNTRY, CALIFORNIA;
OPPOSITE: DANIEL LIEBERMANN, FLYNN McCONE RESIDENCE, SAN RAFAEL, CALIFORNIA

ACADEMY EDITIONS • LONDON

Acknowledgements

All material is courtesy of the architects unless otherwise stated.
We would like to thank Jack Golden of the Friends of Kebyar, Portland, Oregon, for
his support. Thanks also go to Sidney Robinson for his contribution. The office of
Imre Makovecz were extremely helpful and we are indebted to them. We are
grateful to Dennis Hoppen for his enthusiasm. Further thanks are extended to Silvio
Caputo and Clare Brass for obtaining material for publication on Nari Gandhi.

Photographic Credits
Mike Bry *pp2, 69 (above)*; Martin Grummer *p73 (above)*; John Macsai *pp12-13*; Malak Photographs Ltd *p8*; Michael
Moore *pp50-51*; Jay Mroczek *pp66-68, 69 (below)*; Ianthe Ruthven *pp92-96*; Alan Weintraub *p71 (centre)*; Lewis
Wilson *pp72, 73 (below)*; Charlotte Wood *pp20, 24-28*; Scot Zimmerman *pp3, 58-65*; Wade Zimmerman *Cover, pp56-57*;
Tibor Zsitva *p45*

*FRONT COVER: Lester Korzilius, Sylvan Hill Country Residence, Connecticut; BACK COVER: Imre Makovecz,
Original Sketch of Paks Catholic Church; INSIDE COVERS: James T Hubbell, Hubbell Residence, San Diego,
California, detail of mosaic floor*

HOUSE EDITOR: Maggie Toy EDITORIAL TEAM: Nicola Hodges, Katherine MacInnes, Natasha Robertson
SENIOR DESIGNER: Andrea Bettella DESIGN CO-ORDINATOR: Mario Bettella
DESIGN TEAM: Owen Thomas, Jacqueline Grosvenor, Jason Rigby

CONSULTANTS: Catherine Cooke, Terry Farrell, Kenneth Frampton, Charles Jencks
Heinrich Klotz, Leon Krier, Robert Maxwell, Demetri Porphyrios, Kenneth Powell, Colin Rowe, Derek Walker

First published in Great Britain in 1993 by *Architectural Design* an imprint of
ACADEMY GROUP LTD, 42 LEINSTER GARDENS, LONDON W2 3AN
ERNST & SOHN, HOHENZOLLERNDAMM 170, D-1000 BERLIN 31
Members of the VCH Publishing Group
ISBN: 1-85490-237-7 (UK)

Architectural Design Profile 106 is published as part of *Architectural Design* Vol 63 11-12/1993
Architectural Design Magazine is published six times a year and is available by subscription

Distributed in the United States of America by
ST MARTIN'S PRESS, 175 FIFTH AVENUE, NEW YORK, NY 10010

Printed and bound in Italy

Contents

ARCHITECTURAL DESIGN PROFILE No 106
ORGANIC ARCHITECTURE

MAGGIE TOY
ORGANIC ARCHITECTURE
Subtlety and Power

At a time when planet Earth, despite the 'green revolution', is undergoing seemingly irrevocable ecological breakdown, it is pertinent to consider architecture which makes an attempt to avoid apocalyptical conclusions. Some aspects of progress manifested in short-term priorities conceived for the service of the world market are incompatible, impairing the natural balances essential to our survival. Trees continue to be felled to make way for cattle herding and forced cultivation. The earth is a time bomb; the only certainty is that it will explode. But there is time to change things, time to redress the balance and to respond positively. 'Organic' architecture which is linked to green and sustainable development demonstrates, quietly and confidently, a way forward. Here a more harmonious art is being created. Whilst monumental architecture from its beginnings is associated with a profligate attitude towards resources, organic architecture utilises available materials, communing with both the economics of the situation and sustainability.

No matter how many diverse styles become popular at any one time, building forms which resist imposition of the right angle continue to engender response. Organic architecture achieves its power through subtlety and presence with a sense of flowing space. Frank Lloyd Wright, a key exponent, expanded the spatial frontiers of architecture into curved and warped space. This form of architecture realises a significant empathy and bond with nature: designs which are not a conquest of nature but a symbiotic embrace.

Sidney Robinson considers the organic movement in context. Placing modern day exponents in relation to historical influences, he asserts that organic architecture is a challenge to complacency and insists on renewal, and therefore on the impulse of the individual; its tolerance for pursuit rather than certainty, its delight in argument and its rebirth all contribute to its rhetorical rather than philosophical status. Imre Makovecz has effected considerable impact on architecture. His wonderful structures possess the ability to free the mind and facilitate the fantastical. Associated groups that have developed in Hungary alongside Makovecz have combined to produce an internationally influential, regional organic architecture. The latter's forthright and influential views have inspired a generation to join in the creation of a national style.

Ensouling buildings is the preoccupation of Christopher Day who delights in heartfelt curved lines and in the ability of the building to breathe and instil its totality, superseding appreciation through analysis of separate parts. This aspect is pervasive in organic architecture. For one to feel the pulse of a building is important for Day, who consequently produces an organic architecture from within.

The inclusion of Greg Lynn's essay provokes a different train of thought and wards off 'wholesome' organic architecture – buildings, after all, are not organisms but organs, provisional structures which are already multiplicitous. To disentangle the pact between organic bodies and exact geometric language that underlies architecture's spatial types is a monumental task. Architectural proportion achieves the transcendental status of an abstract, holistic organic body, adopting the logic of an organism. Architecture frequently invokes the paradigm of the inviolate interior of a living body. Lynn makes a plea for us not just to accept the superficial, but to analyse the reality of what we see.

Many of these architects tend to move away from mechanical means of illustrating and 'producing' their designs. Buildings are not necessarily drawn before construction begins but rather the forms marked out on site to indicate how they should 'grow'. Many details are developed in situ ensuring full exploitation of the location. In the case of Nari Ghandi, as with many of the architects featured here, drawings are produced after completion for building regulations' permission. The final form can only be ascertained when construction is complete, a process heavy with trust and expectation.

With the recent surge of interest in chaos theory and natural phenomena there comes a wider variety of 'organic' interpretations: featured projects range from Camouflage by Doug Garofalo to the 'breathing' buildings of James T Hubbell; from Terry Brown's sinuous sculpture to the rock formations of John Lautner. The categorisation is held together by the intent to create a sympathetic environment.

Has progress in the modern world taken a wrong turn? Jean Jacques Rousseau posits that man is happier when working directly on the land and this happiness is inversely proportional to his distance from it. This issue is tackled by the architects here and what emerges is a positive message: that a firm belief in collaboration with the environment exists. Perhaps a valid path for the future is to explore the truth and cultivate the virtue which can be gleaned from organic architecture.

OPPOSITE: Daniel Liebermann, working model for ski resort community, Steamboat Springs Colorado, 1979

SIDNEY K ROBINSON
BUILDING AS IF IN EDEN

Organic architecture is a challenge. It challenges architectural conventions and it dares to be pinned down. Taking on the old problem of definition is the only way to engage this elusive phenomenon. Re-definition and the organic are similarly recursive. (Ontogeny repeats phylogeny history of the individual re-enacts the history of the species.) This time, but not for all time, we present a range of sizes, materials, and locations to establish an organic architecture: the Canadian architect Douglas Cardinal's Canadian Museum of Civilization in Hull, Quebec (1990), the Hungarian Gyorgy Csete's artesian spring enclosure in Orfu (1970), and the American Terry Brown's Studio in Cincinnati, Ohio (1993).

Organic architecture is rhetorical. That is why we must start with definition. That is why the words in the title of this article, 'as if' are the crucial ones not the familiar 'Eden', which conventionally gets capitalised. Unreflective notions of the natural or the original must be left behind to open the organic to a wider audience, and to assure that it is a hardy species. Asserting the rhetorical status of organic architecture is liable to upset both those who believe in a unique relation between philosophical classicism and rhetoric, as well as those who believe that organic architecture is beyond such argument. There is nothing self-evident about Eden; it did not exist until we named it in the records of cultures and in the longings of individuals. In the attempt to make Eden an argument, not a place, there is more than a little exhortation in what follows.

Without the bold assertion of a rhetorical status, all we could do for the remainder of this article would be to describe self-identified examples of organic architecture; and repeated description is nothing more than mindless caressing. The buffeting of an idea to strengthen it is comparable to the pressure of climate and predators to ensure the survival of an organism; rhetoric and organic might be seen as parallel in this way. Description and argument will work together from here on.

Douglas Cardinal's Canadian Museum of Civilization comprises two large structures. The million square feet are divided between the Glacier wing and the Canadian Shield (rock formation) wing. At the outset, these names indicate the complex relationship organic architecture has with both the natural world and the human world. The apparent contradiction of housing cultural artefacts in build-ings named for geological phenomena recognises that human life is in fact supported by the earth. One does come before the other.

The size of The Canadian Museum of Civilization helps to make the connection with geological phenomena. Nature is somehow at the heart of organic architecture, but as a referent, not an origin. This architectural statement can hardly be mistaken for a product of nature. It is obviously a human construction even when the architect describes his architectural forms as being 'sculpted by the winds, rivers, the glaciers'.

Familiar conventions include level floors, the better to facilitate walking upright in our naturally unstable position; an economy of effort that pro-duces floor heights in a fairly narrow range (except with mechanical means of escalators and lifts); and a constructional economy that produces repeatable structural elements. But architectural elements like walls and roofs are freer to depart from more conventional ideas of buildings.

The direct association of organic architecture with nature is not generalised. Only some forms of nature are given particular attention. As compared to animals, geological formations or plants do not look back at us. (Insects may be in an ambiguous position in this distinction.) To that degree they do not have a face, which makes face-to-face rhetorical exchange difficult, but not, I submit, impossible. Although Cardinal's buildings have places to enter, they do not have proper facades. The location between street and river suggests they open at least to two worlds, man's and nature's. The plaza that connects the two worlds, as well as the two buildings, has numerous openings for air, light, cars and people.

Cars seem to be an intrusion on the notion of organic architecture. Since there were (are?) no cars in Eden, their appearance here in a 500 car garage under the plaza can only be seen as a critical lapse all too familiar in such a wishful ideal. The charge of inconsistency can be blunted only by acknowledging that making a building that ad-dresses nature cannot escape the 'as if' condition of rhetorical argument. Any rejection of such a move immediately keeps the whole idea of the organic in retreat. Granting that organic architecture's claims depend on its being somewhat off centre, it must be remembered that being on the margin is not the same as being on the run.

OPPOSITE: Douglas Cardinal, the entrance hall of The Canadian Museum of Civilisation, Hull, Quebec, with a view of Parliament Hill across the Ottawa River

The Canadian Museum of Civilization may be too big to be considered organic. The 'intrusion' of technology at this scale apparently removes it from Eden where only the primitive is possible. Anyone who moves through the museum cannot help but be aware of the many ways that the architect uses whatever means, including technology, to make a point about another way of building. We have long ago gone beyond the Bauhaus notion that a building that includes technology must look like a machine, especially 85 non-visible electronics replace pistons and gears. So when we see the waterfall along the stairs between the Glacier Wing and the Canadian Shield Wing, we are not offended. Of course this is driven by a pump, just like any good Picturesque waterfall of 18th-century England. Technology, in any form, drives the organic into the rhetorical mode. To build is to not live like the lilies of the field, therefore it is a propositional activity filled with intention, ideals, structures of meaning.

The sign of the organic in The Canadian Museum of Civilization is the non-rectilinearity of the plan and some of the sections. Walls that are not flat are difficult to approach as facades. The curved perimeter is one of the most obvious and powerful ways to keep the visual intersection from coming to a halt. Continuous surfaces that fade around the bend put off direct engagement. This one fact is probably the most irritating to someone steeped in a convention of direct, positivist encounter. How can you trust something that is trying to make a point if it keeps turning away? That characterisation of a rhetorical encounter is so seriously flawed as to be ludicrous. Rhetoric is so much about adjustments, subtleties, responses to audience and message, that it is often accused, as it was by Plato, of being slippery and unreliable.

So Douglas Cardinal, the lover of curves, keeps the walls moving. He also keeps the expected vertical continuity of walls from lining up. By stepping the layers of floor and window bands in and out, and displacing the curves from layer to layer, the conventions of facade are further undermined. All we have to do to see how powerful are these straightforward moves (if you will permit such a contradiction), is to imagine Cardinal's plans as rectilinear, and the walls all lined up vertically. On one level, the resulting buildings would be topologically the same, but something would obviously be missing. The difference may be something added, but only in the sense that figures of speech are 'added' to discourse. The assumption that some kind of 'plain speech is the bearer of trustworthy facts is surely not supportable. The attempt to assure that what you see is what you get, that appearance guarantees content, permits only statements of self-evident facts, not a dialogue designed to convince.

The tops of the buildings and the tops of the major rooms of The Canadian Museum of Civilization also depart from conventional expectation. Along with plan curves and flowing elevations, the upper boundaries of the buildings rise and fall, and gather into closed, centralised dome-like profiles. Cornices (if you will excuse the expression), or rooflines, and ceilings, free from direct physical contact with people, are probably the most powerful sites for departing from conventional rectilinear references. In The Canadian Museum of Civilization, Cardinal has freely modelled these edges even when the roof behind them is decidedly flat. The desire to integrate the ribbed copper domical roofs into the flowing composition is another reason for the undulating skylines. The line that buildings make with the sky is the most powerful boundary that organic architecture can exploit. Aside from the jobs of keeping water out of the interiors and distributing structural loads around them, the roof/cornice-line is free to participate in an argument that a building can be like the hills, the trees and the clouds.

On the interior, the centralised or axial spaces are capped by smoothly contoured surfaces, lighted at their lower edges so as to make the containment less insistent and determinative. Such ceilings reinforce some idea of centre, as much as they are a way to reinforce the power of the continuously flowing edges.

In Eden, or rather on its threshold, building materials come rather directly from the natural world, whether animal, vegetable or mineral. In such a large building as The Canadian Museum of Civilization, with its expected high traffic volumes, it stands to reason that, like the entrance to a national park, a truly delicate primitiveness would not survive. The limestone, copper and concrete, all from the mineral side of the organic, are rational choices for the buildings' materials. The fossils in the stone help associate the careful laying up of the walls with another world. The flowing surfaces do not emphasise the assembly of the materials whose individualities are subsumed to the sense of the whole. The curves that unite the various materials reinforce the appearance of continuous resistance to the abrasion of moving fluids.

Rock and water and wind. Calling on these natural forces, a little like Lear in the storm, could be dismissed as another instance of the pathetic fallacy. But that is to get it exactly the wrong way round. To paraphrase CS Lewis in his essay on Milton's *Paradise Lost*, ' . . . the possible Paradise Lost in myself interests me more than the possible me in Paradise Lost'. The latter statement turns the pathetic fallacy around by looking for the continuities coming from the earth into us rather than our projection of ourselves onto the earth. It suggests that one can keep one's place even as one picks up the continuity between oneself and forces and forms beyond oneself. Organic architecture tunes its ear to pick up those harmonies and translates them into structures that remind us of that continuity. When the

Alden B Dow, residence, Midland, Michigan, interior of lobby

fallacy is turned around and the translation is understood, we are a long way from adolescent wish fulfilment and self-delusion.

At the other end of the range of organic architecture from the huge museum in Canada is Gyorgy Csete's artesian well enclosure in Hungary. Here in the woods he marks a singular natural phenomenon by prolonging the axis of gravity and the water's resistance to it, while capturing the water for human use.

The concrete of the reservoir at the base of this vessel continues up into the 'house' part as a supporting stem. The steeply pitched wooden roof is capped by a faceted glass bulb where light pours down along the same axis. Textures of form-work and wooden boards are ornamented by very simplified cut-outs with a classical vernacular origin The whole structure looks like some kind of bottle or vase, and what could be more primordial than a vessel for holding water.

Nature's growth and change are in large part supported by water, which has a very different interaction with rocks than with plants. While Douglas Cardinal cited the flowing patterns that result from the interaction of water and rock, Csete, working from the vegetable end of nature, uses wooden planks to create an aspiring, bud-like form produced by the transformation of water by plants. While rock and water produce forms that are direct records of their interaction, plants, and even more so, animals, although they are overwhelmingly constituted by water, do not look like water. Its form, or the evidence of its presence, is substantially translated by its cooperation in the process of birth, growth and death.

Csete, as the leader of the Pécs group of Hungarian organic architects, draws inchoate forces of nature into a unified shape. An artesian spring in the woods can scarcely be surpassed as a site for organic architecture. Rising as if by magic, water overcomes the pull of gravity to burst from the dark earth into the light. The rising force, the contrast between dark and light, the wood and 'liquid stone' (concrete) flow together to create a powerful experience. The smaller scale of the building makes the pieces, whose sizes are determined by the scale of both trees and hands, retain some independent identity. We are aware of the assemblage of materials in producing one of Ruskin's awkward, but nonetheless onomatopoetic words, 'membrification'. A construction's singularity is made provisional by the assertion of the pieces of which it is made. These pieces approach texture, not limbs: in the sense that a tree is largely texture while a donkey is not.

Eden is the time and place before differences appear. Distinctions lie outside the all-embracing continuity. The Garden represents unarticulated abundance and endless potential. Speech, and argument, are not necessary to bridge between things because everything is in touch with everything. If there is a boundary it is only around all,

which is completely interconnected. Nothing is discrete. Boundaries between the 'parts' are not closed, but open.

Organic architecture seeks to build as if in this condition. 'Gardens never end and buildings never begin' as Alden Dow said of his own house and studio in Midland, Michigan, begun in 1935. The constructions are open, they reach out, or prolong forces and forms that surround them. They are aspiring, and in this there is some connection with the Gothic spirit whose roots seem to lie in the non-classical North and East. Here too lies the home of Dionysus whose rites in the forests with fennel rods trimmed with ivy, with fawnskins and flowing hair, instil an ecstasy of merging and unification. The feeling of freedom, of the absence of constraint separating one thing or place or behaviour from another is not meant to replace the world of distinction. After all, the Bacchants feel this way together, not in private.

Organic architecture puts pressure on convention by addressing itself to a specific audience. When it stands out in the crowd of the timid and the tired, it is not just thumbing its nose, trying to make people uncomfortable. It is an open invitation to everyone, not just those most learned in the rules of convention. The argument of organic architecture, like the rites of Dionysus, takes place in a civil society. Its mode of address is distinctive because it is not an issue of faces, but more like glances and hints which have their own structure, to be sure. If nothing else, organic architecture is about renewal, including the continuing necessity to renew conventions. Without challenges, architectural conventions become rigid and fit only for museums or books.

Inside Eden there is only family, blood relationships, feelings of kinship that do not need to be articulated. Outside Eden there is society linked by articulated, negotiated relationships. As Hanna Arendt characterises them, it is like sitting around a table which links even as its separates. As long as the rhetorical stance is rejected, the organic is condemned to wander aimlessly in an allusion of blood ties, unable to present itself and its challenge in a convincing way. Such avoidance of differences also opens it to distortion by appeals to soil, blood and faith in the darkness of ethnic exclusion. Without a rhetorical mode, organic architecture can imagine escaping responsibility for this perversion.

Nonetheless, the family is a powerful model for a particular aspect of the organic. Families outside Eden exist in a civil society. One of the challenges of raising a child is the preparation for adding the articulated world of society to the continuous relationship within the family. It is not a case of replacement, but of expansion. A child learns to work with the conflicting need for both belonging and separation. The one serves as the ground for the other, just as the earth supports culture. The familial support is in the background, an all-pervading assumption which allows, even encourages, its

Alden B Dow, residence, Midland, Michigan

own redefinition. Organic architecture posits a similarly pervasive continuity that supports distinctions. The earth is the great support and buildings that engage it are reminders. Disregarding that great support puts all our artefacts at risk.

Terry Brown's studio, which is under construction in Cincinnati, Ohio, is not large, and it is not marking a place on the earth. It is a place for work, that most human activity. A place for work is the clearest instance of the conjunction of earth and artefact. It is a statement, a challenge, an alternative. The joyfulness of the work is inescapable.

On one of the many hill sides in the river town of Cincinnati, Brown has taken a very conventional small frame house on a corner lot and transformed it. Much of his work up to now has been to start from an existing condition and coax it to another plane. In the centre of the studio complex is the existing house. To back and front are the pavilions added by the architect. They are so unmistakably bud-like in general form as to associate them with natural phenomena. But they also resonate with primitive shelters that gather structural supports at a centre point, top and bottom. The 'as if' condition of organic architecture does not deceive itself with the comfortable self-reference of canonised architectural convention. It knowingly reaches beyond 'architecture' as a gesture towards the 'other' which is the earth.

On the ground, Brown plants three volumes that are like bodies adorned with ornament. These mantles, or even costumes, if you will break out from simply closed boundaries. These bodies support the openings, visors, the efflorescence of structure that is like the flora and fauna articulating and ornamenting the surface of the great body Earth.

These Dionysian dancers, whirling on their axes, fling out their garments in joyful abandon. They are embracing the paradox ER Dodds ascribes to the Dionysian rites. 'Forget the difference, and you will find the identity' if ever there were an 'as if in Eden' proposition, this is surely it.

The materials of Brown's studio flowing courses of shingles, masonry, glass, metal in sheets, rods and frames, are peculiarly part of organic architecture. Materiality is such a central issue for this architecture that we often identify the unexpected, idiosyncratic and sometimes painfully striking use of all kinds of materials as indicative of the organic. Making use of the unconventional, the unexpected is one way to make something new. New is not just a ploy used by fashion, it is also an important way to embody the organic fact of rebirth. At one and the same time, organic architecture points away from itself towards forms and forces beyond it, even as it revels in the intense specificity of its sensory impact. That relationship is a difficult one, to be sure. The Japanese Buddhist aphorism about not mistaking the pointing finger for the moon begins to get at this difficulty.

For organic architecture, matter is not transparent, not something to be seen through on the way to a more abstract reality. Neither is it an idol, a graven image which is magical in and of itself. The material world is all we have, but it is not all there is. Just like the finger and the moon, there is a relationship between this world and Eden. Organic architecture believes there is no possibility of constructing a way to get from here to there. But by acknowledging the gap, it gives independent intensity to both the articulated material indicator and the memory of all embracing continuity. The challenge is to argue continuity by means of discrete constructions without giving up the game and collapsing into the privileged singularity of one or the other.

The argument in which organic architecture is engaged is not pursued with an a priori sense of failure of ever closing the gap. That rejection of failure draws the charge that organic architecture has no tragic sense. Rather than anticipating tragedy, organic architecture greets each day with the same delight as the Spring, embracing both birth and death in their simultaneous continuity. There is no fear of the retribution visited by the gods on either the happy man or on the arrogant man who overstates the isolation and independence of human life (*hubris*). A joyfulness celebrates the continuous shift between the local and the cosmic. To insist on the conclusion of either argument or architectural form is not the point.

The material world is delightful, it is where we are. But it is not self-sufficient. The control of this delight comes from the earth as well: geometry. Geometry from sources other than our orthogonal relationship to gravity is a salient aspect of organic architecture. The great axis between earth and light centralises the bodies of Brown's studio while the flowing gestures of costumes and limbs whirl around it.

Organic architecture is often characterised as anti-intellectual. The claim that it is ultimately rhetorical apparently creates an unbridgeable contradiction. But the suspicion of the mind is a fundamental starting point. The French poet Jacques Prevert said it most trenchantly: *'Quand on le laisse seul, le monde mental, ment monumentalement'*. When left alone, the world of the mind lies monumentally. When the mind asserts its self-sufficiency, organic architecture goes on the attack, joining the march of the Bacchants. The great chain of being must be obeyed. Articulating our place in it is not the same as breaking free of it.

Building as if in Eden is really building on the threshold of the garden. At this intermediate location, the memory of continuity is still fresh, while the doubt that it ever existed has not taken hold. The polarity of difference cannot be accepted. The articulated world outside the garden, expressed by the body, the column, solid and at rest in itself, lies to one side. The brilliant abundance of nature lies on the other. On this threshold attention is alternately outward and inward. Continuous translation of one in terms of the other prevents organic architecture

Gyorgy Csete, Artesian Spring Enclosure, Orfu

from coming to a conclusion or presenting itself as any kind of salvation. Building as if in Eden is not a solution once and for all. Whenever it approaches such a formal style it has just joined the opposition.

By insisting on renewal, organic architecture relies on the impulse of the individual. A building for each person and each place is a proposal made by most organic architects. What could result in a confusion of abundance frightens the philosophies dedicated to controlling abundance by means of rational structures and an internationalism of form, whether columns and pediments or steel sections and glass. Alternatively, the common reference to the earth as the continuous support brings these individual insights into some kind of direction, if not into line. This condition is a cause for anxiousness only in those who require intellectual constructions to be made of one-to-one correlations. Such linking can only occur if there is no abrupt variation in the elements that constitute the argument. Once a gap, as between the finger and the moon is admitted, tight links must give way to a looser, more inclusive composition. That is one difference between philosophy and rhetoric. And that is why organic architecture is rhetorical. Its tolerance for pursuit rather than certainty, its delight in argument and rebirth all contribute to this status.

These three examples of organic architecture have brought out the range of organic architecture. It need not be small in scale, it need not be in a particular place, it need not be irresponsible. Building as if in Eden is a challenge to complacency, which all conventions fall into eventually. There is no expectation that this challenge aims at victory. In that, organic architecture is always on the margin, always the loyal opposition whose quirkiness keeps our eyes open and our spirits uplifted.

Gyorgy Csete, Artesian Spring Enclosure, Orfu

IMRE MAKOVECZ
ANTHROPOMORPHIC ARCHITECTURE
The Borderline between Heaven and Earth

Organic architecture at the beginning was a philosophical and formal question, but it's not merely a philosophical and formal question any more. The world has changed since Frank Lloyd Wright began his work in an organic way and so organic architecture is quite different now. Frank Lloyd Wright's knowledge derived from the 19th century – his teacher was Louis Sullivan – but at the end of the 20th century our problems are quite different. For example; this year in Hungary it was very dry, in Europe there have been windy storms the likes of which no one remembers. Many forests were simply destroyed by these storms. 25 per cent of Hungarian forests have disappeared in the last ten years. Acid rains are coming here from England, Germany and Czechoslovakia. From the east we have the effects of Chernobyl which are changing plants and even human beings, producing mutations. So the whole of nature is being destroyed and is changing very quickly. Parallel to this process, meta-nature, this second nature, has two important components – money and information. In both East and West, societies are going farther and farther away from original nature and an atmosphere of a coming tragedy is gathering. The tragedy of this meta-nature is that it does not recognise that human beings have an original 'created' nature in themselves. The body, the whole human way of living, is part of that original nature.

Those who think they understand architecture usually approach organic architecture in terms of 'form'. But in viewing the architecture of Frank Lloyd Wright, Bruce Goff, Herb Greene, Rudolf Steiner, Lechner Ödön, Antoni Gaudí, Kós Károly or William Morris we are looking at completely different worlds from the point of view of form. I think it is the *mode of thinking* or their *view of life* which makes these people representatives of organic architecture. One of the significant things about this view is that they are searching for metaphors between the meta-nature of society and the created world. The abyss which opens again and again between these two is unbearable for them. To this end, Gaudí and Morris used plant metaphors, Greene used animal metaphors and Rudolf Steiner used human metaphors. It was absolutely essential for these architects to view the world as a continuity.

My architecture has nothing to do with traditional architecture in the sense of its philosophy and its form. I create this new architecture as a protest about the situation imposed by meta-nature. It doesn't need the Hungarian organic traditions of folk architecture as a way of being 'different', or because it is taking a humanistic or a poetic view. I have a quite different reason why I use it; I use it because of what is shows through feeling-knowledge. It is this knowledge of the cultures of ten, twenty thousand years ago that is very important for us to understand today. It's not a question, for instance, that the culture of the Maoris is very fascinating – it's a question of what they know and what we don't know. What the work of Carl Jung shows is that with an elementary knowledge of the Maoris and the archetypes it is possible to have a very deep inner connection with those people, that is possible to decipher the architecture of two, three, ten thousand years ago. Take the artist Joseph Beuys: it's very important to understand his performance in New York where he spent three days in a room with a coyote, which symbolises the American Indians, the presence of a traditional god. Why did he need to do this? So in the same way, why do I feel I need to use elements of Hungarian folk art? Why is it important for an English architect to understand what is the knowledge behind Stonehenge?

I don't think that the new architecture in Australia needs to derive from the thoughts of the Aborigines; I think that the Australian ancient culture comes from Central Asia, so maybe you have to look for it there. There would be very many sources – it's not necessary that you would have to look for the roots of Australian culture just within Australia. If I were an Australian I would have thought many times about this question, so I haven't got much more I can say about it. For me, in Central Europe, the thing that I am trying to realise is the two great ancient cultures of this area, the Celtic and the Scythian – how they should be understood, sensed or felt in my mind and my heart – I believe that they belong together. Through that I am trying to understand what is happening in Hungary now. And so, I know how hard this task is. I think that architects are now on a borderline and they must decide whether they will serve the coming tragedy or whether they are serving the new 'mythical' society. There are very few architects dealing with so-called 'living architecture', and we are considered as fools or extremists.

For me, notions like individual, community, one's country and the world are petals grown on the same stem, covering each other just like the petals of a rose, not able to be changed or torn out of their original place. For this reason our architecture

OPPOSITE: Farkasrét Cemetery Chapel, Budapest

15

means buildings bound to Man, place surroundings, native country, Europe and Earth. The realisation of buildings bound to Man, surroundings and native country requires the transformation of the intermediary information systems and expanding the possibilities of form and material. What I believe to be the most important concern of this architecture is the drama of our activities.

I had to design a church in a little Hungarian town called Paks where there is a nuclear reactor. A whole district was created around this nuclear reactor, with socialistic ideas of town planning. And so I had to work out what this church should be like and this was quite a problem. A Catholic church in that environment is anachronistic, but nevertheless I wanted to create a space which had a positive effect on the people, a protectiveness – not in its ideology, not in its form or style, but in its reality. I think that it is the duty of every building to be a protection against the many attacks from the outside world, against rain and wind, the cold, from the many radiations which are both positive and negative. There is nothing special in this protectiveness. But there is a great difference between whether this protection comes about through a flat, reinforced concrete surface, or whether through a cupola, as in the case of the culture house in the forest of Visegrád. This has foliated columns and zodiac signs, the columns and zodiac signs of which are not just something theatrical but help to realise inwardly what is in the surrounding cosmos. In that realisation there is a special kind of protection.

What would be the solution for large collections of dwellings in a big city? Here we must ask: why are there 22 million people now living in flats in Mexico City, why has London become a country in itself? Why are there two million people living in Budapest? The villages stand empty in Hungary, people are leaving their traditional abodes. It is true that today it is impossible to live in the countryside and it is only possible to live the cities? Nevertheless, when people go to Milan, or Stockholm, they are not admiring the big living estates; when they go to London they are only admiring the historical old town-centre, which is different from any other town-centre. I said before that at the end of the 20th century, meta-nature is controlled by money and information. Who told people that they must live like this?

In a town called Sárospatak a number of us here have collaborated to design new dwellings to help strengthen the small town atmosphere. The buildings are not more than three floors, so people are in contact more directly with the earth and do not feel like they are rats in a box. I thought it was good to give the task of designing different buildings to different architects, so the buildings would have different faces.

It is important that architecture develop not by satisfying its historical narcissism or generic limitations, but by giving shape to a universal spirit.

My concern is with the way that spirit is incarnated through the human body and appears in the shape of the Hungarian metaphor. This is anthropomorphic architecture, but in truth it is anthropomorphic only in the same way that human speech is possible with the help of the mouth and throat. This architecture creates a world of lifelike objects somewhere on the borderline between heaven and earth. It is meant to be the new alternative: life lived consciously, closer to a new frontier.
(Extracts from an interview with Imre Makovezc by Nigel Hoffmann, first published in Transforming Art, *1991, No 5 Sydney.)*

Paks Catholic Church, 1987

Roots of Hungarian 'Living Architecture'

Imre Makovecz is generally acknowledged as the originator of a distinct Hungarian architectural phenomenon known as 'organic' architecture or 'living architecture'. Especially outside his native country he has been recognised both for his distinctive architecture and his inspired demonstration to others of native roots. He is conscious of his leadership role, both as spokesman and as exemplar.

When viewed from outside Hungary, Makovecz seems like a unique artistic giant of originality and dedication. Without depreciating the difficulty of working creatively within a tiny and economically restrained socialistic country and without challenging Makovecz' continuously heroic activities, he is one of many architects so dedicated. It is a phenomenon that must be appreciated within his native context.

Hungary as a political entity has a long history of oppression from outsiders in which native culture has had a critical role in maintaining national identity. Among the most admired architectural roots are Ödön Lechner (1845-1914) who has been called the Hungarian Gaudí. Lechner won national competitions for the Postal Saving Bank, the Museum of Decorative Art and the Geological Institute, all major public buildings in Budapest. Then there was Karoles Kos (1883-1977) whose National Romanticism was inspired by the most remote Hungarian folk culture in Transylvania, and whose buildings developed a distinct national identity based on traditional materials and forms.

Born on 20th November 1935 in Budapest, Makovecz acknowledges his native beginnings and his slow maturity with occasional creative opportunities in a state architectural office, and his current exceptional entrepreneurship. He exudes the lively enthusiasm that characterises many of his countrymen. Makovecz does not speak English but his native Hungarian is animated and articulate. He has given many interviews and is the accommodating focus of visiting foreign architects and students. As the proprietor of one of the few independent practices in the country he is also among the most creative and original architects. There are two other qualified architects in his 'creative studio' office. In addition, he uses and interacts with a secondary support studio.

In Hungary architectural fees are 1.5 per cent of the construction cost. Last year he grossed 2.5 million forints in fees for 10,000 to 20,000 metres squared of buildings. (Government controlled architectural offices typically produce 30,000 to 40,000 metres squared of building per year. Average construction costs are 7,000 forints per metre squared.)

European colleagues don't know how he survives either financially or creatively. His overhead is about 55 per cent. That includes taxes, medical insurance and other benefits. Architects in Hungary are paid an average of 6600 forints per month – about $1,500 US – but conversions do not accurately reflect costs and buying power.

Unlike architectural offices in both socialist countries and capitalistic countries. Makovecz out of principle refuses to put his employees on fixed salaries, or on pay schedules based on economic output. He believes that such a method of reward destroys the meaning of work for architects. In spite of the potential conflict Makovecz tries to balance staff pay with needs as well as productivity. Thus an architect with two babies at home may be paid more than the value of his current work because of his needs. Such concern for the human element he believes is fundamental to the conception of organic architecture. Makovecz' colleagues come to work with him for very special and dedicated reasons, and he tries to support that commitment.

Makovecz graduated from the University of Technology of Budapest in 1960 – the only professional Hungarian school in a country of ten million inhabitants and the size of Indiana. At the age of 20 or 21 he discovered Frank Lloyd Wright. He read everything he could get his hands on – which in the Hungary of that time was not easy. He studied every illustration. Next in terms of influence came Rudolph Steiner and his Goetheanum near Basel in Switzerland. Makovecz was still studying architecture at the University when he saw pictures of Herb Greene's house outside Norman, Oklahoma that was finished in 1961. Like others he saw not just its animalistic form and natural materials, but also those primordial elements like the great eye that overlooked the prairie. Makovecz says that his own ski house of 1980 follows the design of Herb Greene's house.

Makovecz remembers the exhilaration of discovering how the ancient language of architecture was buried within the Hungarian tongue. Words that describe building parts in fact are anthropomorphic. The ridge is the 'spine'. Doors are 'wings'. Timbers and rafters are 'horns'. Windows are 'eyes'. Eyebrows, forehead and forelock all have exact architectural meaning, and outdoor space is 'life' itself. He suggests at best we can only use our imagination to compose a whole building from these words of fragmentary meaning of some prehistoric age: a complete house that integrates all

these parts – some legendary half human, half animal shelter that houses the most complete human memory and conscience. Our test as architects is to discover that form.

Makovecz believes that architecture anywhere is a serious and profound responsibility. He sees the games of the Best Stores designs in the USA and the ironies of Charles Moore as both cruel and destructive. To build fake ruins as unrooted forms, reveals a society that neglects its own traditions and avoids inner human purity.

Makovecz has both simple and strong ideas about architecture, and a powerful personality that attracts belief. He inspires community effort and team participation both in aligning programmatic commitments and in galvanising physical action. Such effective leadership away from the drawing board has accounted considerably for his success in getting project built. It is probably revealing that he has almost nothing built in Budapest, the capital. His most interesting and most important designs have been built in remote locations, small villages, university towns and hereto unimportant minor centres.

Makovecz' concern with the spirit of the place and the need for architecture to be connected with the particular is part of the reason he has accepted such commissions that ambitious or name architects might reject. He has thus worked without fee but some exchange of food for clients in distant and poor villages, and for clients whether individual or collective who have the most modest of resources. Sometimes meagre budgeted and crude craftsmanship challenge the concept and depreciate the results. On other occasions physical and financial deprivation result in meaningful and memorable architecture.

The community of Zalaszentlaszlo was such a test. With almost no building budget the villagers themselves went to the edge of the settlement, cut the trees and dragged the trimmed trunks to the site. There they became trees again in a new context. The wooden colonnade embraces a refurbished farmhouse – itself abandoned because it was the home of a Jewish family who were hauled away and killed during the last war. Their spirits are now alive again in a community meeting space and pub. The live spirits of the trees come from the mountain to embrace the house, to guard against such stupidities in the future. Here lack of money was compensated by intensity of need. But it was built from the most insignificant of materials. For reasons of both concept and economy their architecture is built of traditional and domestic materials, often using traditional structural systems and joining materials. Timber frame, wood boarding, tile or thatch roof, and wet plaster are characteristic.

The style that emerges from the use of such technology may be similar in many buildings and may seem to be trite in terms of the inherent values of the parts. For Makovecz the role of the architect is

Sárospatak Culture Centre, 1974-83

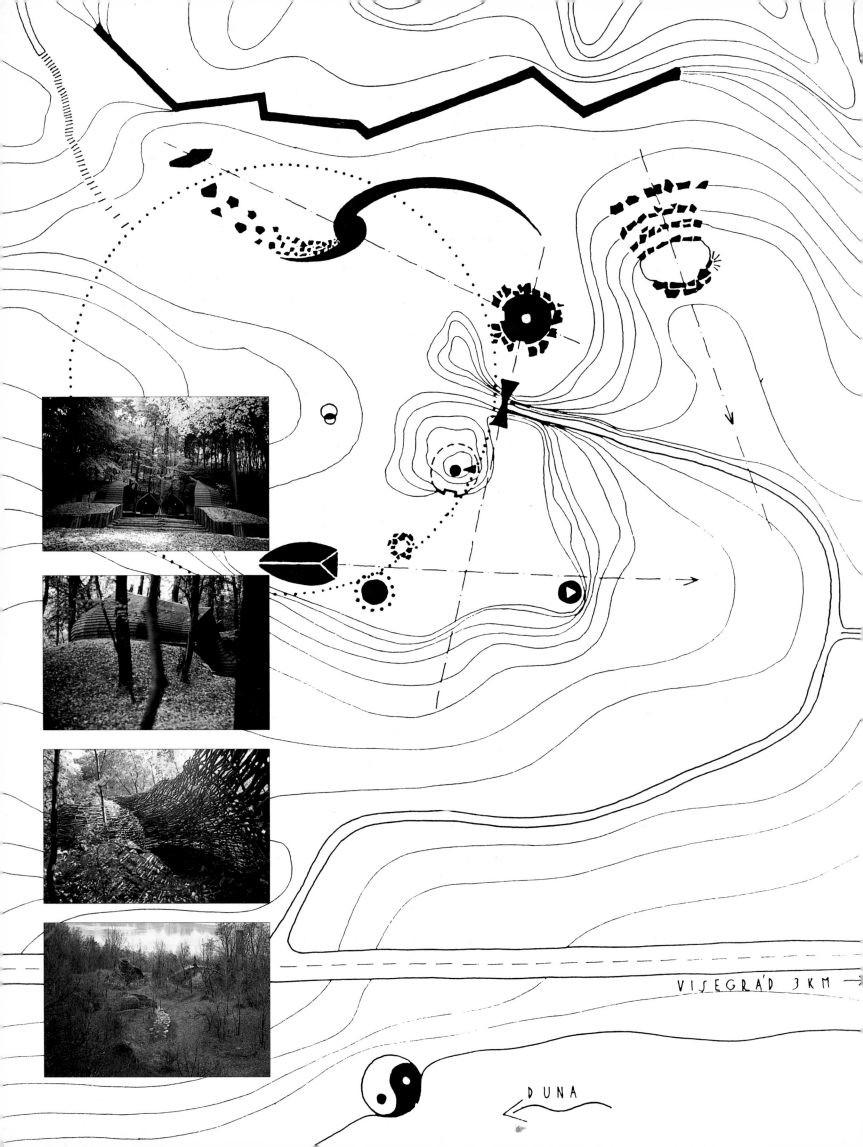

VISEGRÁD 3KM

DUNA

not in the cost of construction materials, or the clever techniques of their assembly. Rather, it is to celebrate, to transform and to dramatise daily life.

In contrast modern architecture provides many examples of lifeless built form. Makovecz can look across the Danube to see the flash of modern International Style hotels at prime locations on the banks of a beautiful river. They are built with foreign capital. They must be repaid with foreign capital, and they cater to foreigners. Natives don't go there because they don't provide for local needs. In addition they make local people feel uncomfortable. Natives also cannot afford them. These hotels are indeed foreign, and are multiple losers for local life and local economy.

Makovecz began very much as a rural boy. In the Hungarian countryside his childhood included the terrifying memories of events before, during and after the Second World War. He was ten in 1945. He remembers how the farmers had to survive after their fields were cleared, all their produce was taken away and their animals stolen. He remembers the family farm of about two acres after the first land reform when it was slightly larger than before. Then the farm was absorbed into a collective farm. After some years some of the fields were returned. Then they were lost never to be returned. He remembers as a child being put on a strange couch in some anonymous shelter and instructed to do as he was told. And he remembers the even more touching terrors of others. They were hard years to believe in the goodness of living.

Makovecz sees Hungary today as a different place but still with a legacy of ruthlessness. He together with many other Hungarian architects criticises the endless apartment blocks built in the 1960s and 1970s. While they provide accommodation they also regulate lives in a totally mechanical pattern. All have the same small balcony. All buildings have the same orientation. It has nothing to do with the sun and rarely bears much relationship to site. Every individual apartment has the same plan. The family size is the same. The TV will sit only in one place. Every evening throughout the country people sit facing in the same position – all the lines of television viewing are polarised by the architecture of the room layout and land planning. They are buildings with a minimalist mentality. They are easy to build and easy to operate. Simultaneously, they provide social isolation and acoustic amplification. On the third floor you can hear a family quarrel on the first floor.

Such environments are often called International Style and blamed on the Bauhaus. Yet, Makovecz respects the creativity and liveliness of the Bauhaus inspired architecture in Hungary before the Second World War. He obviously knows their work well. He notes that unfortunately current official architecture is very selective in its antecedents. Certain prominent historic architects are persistently not published, and earlier books about their works have long since been out of print. He accuses art and architectural historians of not being politically alive enough to get the full richness of the past published.

Makovecz clearly sees and talks about style as a system of thinking and not a pattern of forms. Now he believes that International Style Architecture is truly dead. It has no reality in the late 20th century. Only the Armenians, the Jews and Palestinians may be international cultures – to the extent that they are homeless and transient people and have no roots. But of course International Style Architecture is even more meaningless for them.

Makovecz is proud of his leadership of the now living architecture of the organic in Hungary. But he is hardly vain about his position. He jokes about his personal life but not about architecture. He recognises a certain consistency, perhaps persistence in his own design. He tries not to copy himself. But after the 15th house that attempts to be creative by going back to basics, the result may not be so unique. Inevitably what you did before will influence what follows. As a child learns to write by using a copy book with guidelines, so an architect following similar thought patterns will produce identifiable results. For himself Makovecz would like to continue the architectural search for creative contact with reality, with the world of human life and its most memorable meaning and origins.

Makovecz like other organic architects has received his most significant professional notice outside his own country – a recognition pattern that continuously rubs salt into the more official and international style architects of Hungary. Already in 1968 Makovecz was awarded the YBL prize for his restaurant in Tatabanya that reintroduced folk heritage into Hungarian architecture. The prize is the most coveted national honour for an Hungarian architect and is named after Nicholas Ybl, a famous neo-Renaissance architect of the late 19th century. Only recently Makovecz has been recognised by inclusion in the Hungarian architectural and cultural press. His work has been exhibited at the Venice Biennale as early as 1973 and the Paris Biennale. In June 1987 the American Institute of Architects awarded him an Honorary Fellowship in the AIA: FAIA (Hon).

(Extracts from a report and conversation with Imre Makovecz by Professor Jeffrey Cook, AIA, Arizona State University, Friends of Kebyar, Vol 5.4.)

ABOVE: Conceptual sketch of the tower at Mogyoróhegy Recreation Park, Visegrád Camp; OPPOSITE, FROM ABOVE: Scenes from the Mogyoróhegy Recreation Park – open-air dining area; shower and toilet block; the 'knot'; view of the campsite; BACKGROUND: Site plan of Mogyoróhegy Recreation Park

CHRISTOPHER DAY
ENSOULING BUILDINGS

Nowadays if you stand in front of, or go into, a new building the usual experience is one of emptiness. It waits for someone to come along and give it love, cosiness, individuality, to put curtains in the windows, flowers on the balcony, life in the rooms. And so it should! Until that someone comes along, however, many buildings are lifeless. They offer nothing other than constraints and architectural qualities – space, light and so on – to build upon, to work together with. Such buildings have not yet started the process of being ensouled.

So what is this process of giving a building a soul?

Soul can incarnate progressively into a building as it progressively gains substance from wish, through idea, planning, constructional design, building and occupation. Each stage develops, deepens and extends that which had come before. They are not stages which alternate from aesthetic to practical but, with these aspects inseparable throughout, are stages of continuous process of incarnation into substance until we architects complete our task, leaving a shell for life which will continue to grow.

It is conspicuous that buildings which have been designed and built without care, or where their tenancy and management structure discourages tenant care, replacing it with dependency on a faceless or exploitive owner, rapidly deteriorate into slums. A generation ago, slums used to mean buildings with physical deficiencies. Today's slums are buildings from which care is absent.

Old buildings are rarely just museums of a particular period of history. They have physical elements from many dates right up to the present and they have the imprint – both visibly and invisibly – of the many occupants, lifestyles and values that inhabited them. When this has been a harmonious progression, the new built upon the past rather than brutally pushing it aside, ripping it out and trampling it, these buildings have charm and appeal.

People choose old buildings to live in. Of course people also choose to live in other sorts of buildings, but for other reasons. What I have described for buildings also applies to landscapes: everything new that we build will be set in a landscape or townscape that already exists and which has been made up by a long historical process. What we tend to call *sites* are already *places,* places to which their histories have given soul and spirit.

The soul of a place is the intangible feeling – made up of so many things – that it conveys. It is for instance sleepy, smells of pine trees, is friendly, airy, quiet, its roads and paths do not hurry but turn slightly so that everything can always be seen anew each time you pass. Upon this composite of sensory experiences, reinforced by historical associations ('under this clock is where couples always met, even my grandparents', 'this is where the great ships were built', etc) we begin to feel that there is something special about this place, unique, living and evolving, but enduring beyond minor change. It is a being in itself. I call this the spirit of a place. Every place should have a spirit; indeed, unless it has been destroyed by brutal unresponsive actions, every place does.

Children know every corner of the little piece of land they play on. It gives them happiness and health forces they will carry into later life. To the small child it is a whole world, every part an individuality and large in area. Revisit it as an adult and it seems tiny. Revisit it as a site manager and 'here we can stack the concrete units, here the reinforcing steel; we need only to level the site first'. Nowadays so much land is *used*, so little *appreciated*.

When we think of projects these days – urban redevelopment, housing estates, motorway junctions, oil terminals, airports – how many places with a special, unique, valuable and health-giving spirit cease to exist? Whenever we build something new we have a responsibility to this spirit of place. A responsibility to add to it. To the Ancient Greeks the sense of these beings was so strong that in particular places they could say 'here lives the god'. They then enclosed and strengthened this being with a temple.

Today our buildings serve different functions – inside and outside ones. *Inside* is to house an idea, say a clinic, a shop, a home. *Outside* they bound, articulate, focus or alter an external space, adding to or detracting from what is already there, the spirit of place. Many outside spaces serve both functions – an 'idea' function (like a meditation garden, private courtyard or car park) and a 'response to place' function.

Because the inside space, activities and qualities of a building and the outside surfaces and appearance are interrelated, the whole building and all the activities it generates need to be involved in this great conversation. The conversation between idea, usage and place, between what will be and what already was. Between physical substance – the materialisation of the idea – and invisible spirit of place – the spirit brought into being by the physical substance of the surroundings. This is a fundamental responsibility in any architectural action. At first sight it might seem too big a responsibility to cope with, but I don't approach it like that. What I do first is try to listen to the place, listen to the idea and find ways in which they are at least compatible. At best they can symbiotically reinforce each other. Then I try to design a building which has the appropriate qualities. In a landscape, this often requires a building which is as small in scale as possible. This can be achieved for instance with low eaves, preferably below eye-level, or by tucking the building into the landform or placing it so as to extend or turn the lines of hedgerows or landform features.

Townscape situations have different requirements. Perhaps the critical issue might be to find the right scale and intensity of visible activity while at the same time minimising adverse effects like shading or noise, especially in the more sensitive neighbouring zones. Enclosure, compression, openness, sunlight, activity, vegetation, airways, acoustic textures (like plank pavements) and so on are all things that a place can ask for, that can bring a benefit to what already is. Light (including colour), life (especially vegetation), air quality and noise reduction (especially mechanical acoustic noise, but also sensory, especially visual 'noise') and spatial variety, meaningful to the soul, are likely to be amongst the critical elements.

The building itself needs appropriate qualities which both add to how it looks from outside and colour the *activities* within and around it (these activities may well have a greater impact on the surroundings than the building itself will!) It needs a meaningful choice of materials. Traditionally materials found in the surroundings were raised artistically to become buildings. Today we are free to use anything. But to fit, the materials need to feel right for the place. When I go to a new site, I can feel for example, a stone or a wooden building would be right here; or perhaps for this use, the building needs to assert its purposes a little more and should be rendered block; here it should be more urban in character – brick perhaps?

A building needs forms and shapes – outlines – roof and eaves lines which relate to (not necessarily copy) or perhaps contrast the surroundings. These, combined with plan shape, create the appropriate gestures: of welcome, of privacy, of activity, of repose. These in turn are part of the experience of approaching and entering a building. Roads, paths, boundaries (such as fences or woodland edge) and topographic features (such as the junction of sloping and level land) tie a building into the landscape. The 'keyline' system of erosion control and fertility building is generated from the 'key' topographic meeting point between steep and flattening slope.[1] The placing of woodland, roads and fences is critical. It is no coincidence that these can make a development belong to a place or, if unconsidered, assault it spiritually and ecologically. They are all features which are either already there and anchor that which is new, or are implied by the relationship between the existing situation and the new building.

I notice that, quite unconsciously, I often prefer to locate buildings on the edge of a site where there is something, a wall perhaps or meeting point of different qualities of place, out of which the building can grow. There will also be more open space left on site to do something attractive with, and not just bits of left-over space all around the building.

In built-up areas where open space and sunlight are at such a premium, buildings placed to dominate the site are spatially – and in this commercial world monetarily an extravagance we can rarely afford. Buildings sited to give priority to the place they bound make better environmental and economic sense.

As one approaches a building there is a moment when you come to be aware of the influence of its *activities*. This is a threshold. It is the place for a bridge or archway, either built, formed of trees meeting overhead or implied by buildings compressing and focusing space. There are other ways of giving emphasis to this threshold, like using a turn in the path around a building corner, a group of trees or slope of land, a change in ground surface such as from long to mown grass or gravel to brick paving. Gates and steps are traditional threshold markers.

If we are to bring anything new to a place and make it better, not worse, that new thing must have an artistic quality. Art starts when inspiration struggles with the constraints of matter. When the painter paints, any pre-formed idea has to give way to what is developing on the canvas; matter and spirit become interwoven into a single whole. The idea on its own existed outside the sphere of earthly reality or life – the painting process gives it reality and life.

This process applies as much in architecture as in any other art. First someone perceives a need, sometimes a set of needs; then comes the idea – how to satisfy this need; then an architectural concept; then a building plan, constructional design, a period of building longer and using more energy and money than the previous planning stages; then use – even longer and where the building affects the occupants and users every day!

Conventionally, artistic design stops at or only a little beyond the planning stage. But most of the work is still to come. If any product is to be artistic, the people who make it need to be involved in the artistic process. Of course, builders have not necessarily gone through the same process of developing their aesthetic sensitivities as have architects, but there are other ways to look at it.

It is often said: 'What is wrong with this region is that there is no overall planning!' We live daily in localised experience, all influenced by a regional structure. Our local world is the victim or beneficiary of mega-decisions: after Regional Planning comes District Planning (we begin to *see* the conse-

Nant-y-Cwm, Steiner Kindergarten

quences here) – then architecture. Architects tend to agree how important this is. Then the textures, loving craftsmanship (or otherwise) with which things are built, then building maintenance. Then *homemaking* – both at home and at work – perhaps the most important stage of all that makes places welcoming and our lives a pleasure – or not! If left out, it undoes all the good built up so far.

Generations of care and life give old buildings their charm; lack of it turns them rapidly into slums. The *architectural* qualities have but a small part to play in this spirit that grows up in places. I am reminded of this every time I see an attractive but empty holiday home. Yet it is everything that has gone before that influences whether places will be loved and cared for, or resented and abused. Only for a century or so has this whole process been compartmentalised so that aesthetics is restricted to the architectural stage. Yet great ideas badly, carelessly, lovelessly built are awful to live in! Many qualities depend upon *how* they are made.

Many of the finer qualities of a space – the complexity of meeting forms and planes, the metamorphosis of one shape, form, space into another, the effects of natural and artificial light – can only be approximately and inadequately anticipated. They must be made.

Dead straight lines are so *dead*. To give them life they need to be not wobbly, random or weak but made with a feeling hand. Made. This is the sphere where *only* the building workers can make or break a building. When you make things with your own hands you just can't make *satisfactorily* the same form in different materials. It feels different, needs a different structure and form.

Making and building things is the stage at which idea meets material. They can either compromise each other or, through their fusion, reach a higher level. Sculpture in the mind is pointless. Without art, stone fresh from the quarry is little more than a pile of broken rock. It is, however, a *little* more than just a pile because each material already has something in it waiting to find an appropriate place and form. Not every stone has Michelangelo's *David* in it, but every stone has a quality of 'stoneness'. The violence of the quarry leaves it with sharp split surfaces, but the quality of enduring rock *can* be refound.

All materials have individual qualities. Wood is warm, it has a life to it even though the tree is long felled; brick still has, to touch and to the eye, some of the warmth of the brick kiln; steel is hard, cold, bearing the impress of the hard, powerful industrial machines that rolled or pressed it; plastic has something of the alien molecular technology of which it is made, standing outside the realm of life and, like reinforced concrete, bound by no visible structural rules. It is out of these qualities that materials speak. It is hard to make a cold-feeling room out of unpainted wood, hard to make a warm, soft, approachable room out of concrete.

Materials are the raw ingredients of art. But already they affect our emotions. Mediocre architecture on a scale that is not oppressive is really quite pleasant in timber or a well-chosen brick but a disaster in concrete or asbestos-cement panel.

On the whole, people don't look at architecture, nor at materials. They breathe it in. It provides an atmosphere, not a pictorial scene. When you look at a photograph of an attractive place you notice how much of the picture is ground surface. Our field of vision usually includes more ground than sky. Our feet walk on it. The materials of the ground surface are *at least as important* as those of the walls.

Beyond individual personal preferences we respond to the history and 'being' of the material printed into its appearance. Our feelings are not random but relate to how appropriate this 'being' is to our needs of soul. They also are closely interwoven with the effects that the material has on the body.

Biologically and emotionally metal, reinforced concrete and plastic are not good materials to live within, but wood is – very much so. Nowadays when we think of wood we picture not the curving branches and forks chosen by the shipwrights and early framed-house builders but machine-extruded strips. These lend themselves well to planes but poorly to curves – the opposite of brick where curves can give such strength you can't push over a tall narrow wall. In wood, I usually make curved gestures out of straight lines. Three-facet arches, polygonal spaces give much firmer forms than jigsaw-cut curves. They well suit its softer, more approachable surface. Curves can look silly made up out of planks, but when they are curves of firmness, of structural meaning (as a wooden boat is) then they look really wonderful. I am not averse to curved wood, but the curves need strength. If you steam or cut curves by hand, the limitations of tools and materials give this strength. If you have the freedom of a jig- or band saw, they only will work if you have first learnt with hand tools.

Wood allows longer horizontal runs of windows without any visual loss of structural strength. Sometimes, even, the windows *are* the structure. Wood is for life above the ground. It needs a masonry base to root it in the earth – a heavy inward-leaning base, preferably part-covered with vegetation. The linear characteristics of wood can be exaggerated or softened by colour – white fascias and corner boards emphasise the lines which enclose shapes more than do any other colour (except perhaps yellow or orange). Low pigment stains and, particularly, unstained natural weathering soften the effects of shape. Even very square buildings blend gently into the landscape when they are weathered grey: it is such a life-filled grey, quite unlike grey paint! Unfortunately though, it is not always the best thing for the wood.

Ffald-y-Brenin, Christian Retreat Centre

I don't think that I am alone in feeling at home with natural materials. By 'natural' I mean of course modified nature. The tree is sawn and planed, earth baked into bricks and tiles and so on, but there is still a strong link between finished appearance (and sometimes feel and smell) and natural origins.

Natural materials are 'natural' for human environment. They help to give us roots. The need for roots has led to revivals of past styles of architecture – but, however skilfully they are recreated, when · revivalist forms are built in modern materials – reinforced concrete, glass-reinforced plastic, imitation stone, wood laminates – they look as fake and hollow as they sound when you tap them.

One aspect of traditional building materials is that they are all bound by the scale of the human body: bricks are sized to be laid by hand, prefabricated panels by crane. Compared to ordinary concrete paving slabs (not my favourite material), concrete pavements cast *in situ,* sectioned only by expansion joints, are a huge step away from human scale. A large, simple roof can be at least acceptable if not attractive in subtly variegated tiling but is dominating and place-sterilising if in uniform asphalt.

Anthropometric measurements such as the imperial system, and even more so the ell,[2] imprint the measurements of the body into a building. Our main concern however is how many body heights something is, how much above eye level, how many paces away, how much within or beyond our reach.

When we design things on paper we tend to consider dimensions arithmetically. 2.2 metres is a mere 10 per cent longer than 2 metres. In life, however, we experience dimension anthro-pometrically. A standard door opening is 2 metres high. 10 per cent higher it is almost at (common) ceiling level; we would hardly experience passing under it. 10 per cent lower and – at least psychologically – we need to duck under it. These few centimetres hardly noticeable on the drawing, make all the difference. (We can achieve both safety and threshold experience if we arch the opening so that it is high enough to pass through but feels lower.) Similarly, an inch more or less on the rise of a step makes a dramatic difference to the experience of going up or down stairs.

Small measurements in relation to eye level are critical to views and privacy. A few inches in the height of walls profoundly alters our spatial experience. We also experience objects anthropometrically. We can experience a sugar cube within the hand, and something larger within our arm encompass, but when an object is just a bit bigger so that we can no longer see or feel it without walking round it, we start to experience it differently. Even the smallest buildings like bus-shelters are in this scale, but when designing it is very hard not to draw, model, experience and think of them as immediately comprehensible objects.

How big a building appears in the landscape is affected both by the proportion of roof to wall and by the time of year. Walls confront one whereas the roof slides away and also has a perspective reduction. The gesture of a steep roof can tie a building down to the ground whereas a shallow one with deep eaves can frame and emphasise a wall.

In towns, where views are often so hemmed in that we are not aware of the upper parts of buildings unless we look *along* streets, other factors are involved in perceived scale. Horizontal distance in relationship to event, textural scale and comparative sizes of distinct building units, vegetation and visible sky are more significant. Where we can see them, parapet skylines tend to increase apparent size and therefore 'urban-ness'; visible (therefore fairly steeply-pitched) roofs do the reverse. Where we may wish to reduce *apparent* density, with its close association with crowding stress, we may choose pitched roofs; where city-centre stimulation is a priority, they might not be so appropriate.

Seasonal growth or snow banks can make a striking difference to the apparent scale of things. The walls of traditional buildings with their low doorways and eaves were lower than some annual plants. In some three weeks of early summer or one night of snowfall, such buildings could change from focal points to the barely visible. Human life also, in its relation to the forces of nature, experienced the same dramatic rhythmic swings. Nowadays we have evened out these experiences; enlarging buildings, raising eaves, cultivating low gardens – often only mown grass – and imposing regular patterns of work regardless of season.

Nowadays many people seek to find roots in tradition, in tracing their family histories. The life-renewing rhythms of nature root us in time and place. But how many urban children even know that grass can flower? Every half month has a definably different quality to the preceding and following half month. Almost every week of the year is distinct, yet in many places you can only experience seasons. When I lived in London the months had no individuality – they were just summer and winter.

It is the progression of nature's rhythms in one place that is so rooting, centring, stabilising. Travelling to find seasons – especially out-of-season, such as winter holidays on the beach in Tunisia or early summer skiing in Northern Scandinavia – is like buying vegetables out of season – and as crazily driven by economic reasons. To make money, farmers and market gardeners try to produce food out of season when the price is higher; often by the time the food reaches the kitchen it is hardly recognisable as anything that ever grew in the land – and neither is the tourist hotel in a fishing village or the ski-resort on summer-grazing pasture. To redress this de-rooting of everyday life, I have been asked to design farms where city children can come to experience where food comes from, what happens at what time of year, how it is done, how *they* can do it – to find roots in life.

Places give roots to people, anchors which we

25

need so much in rootless times when one after another codes of behaviour, established institutions, ways of looking at the world are called into question. Personal identity, marriage stability, expectations of employment – all seem so much less certain than they did to our parents.

Buildings threaten and destroy or add to and create places. Their first responsibility must be to add to places, to nurture the spirit of place – which in turn nurtures us. The interiors of buildings also create inner places. Each room has a spirit. It starts with the architecture and develops through usage.

In the dark we can go into two rooms in a strange house – one is a bathroom, one a bedroom. We know instantly which is which; we can hear the acoustic difference. The architectural differences start with the senses. But there can also be rooms with similar spatial characteristics – say two identical prefabricated buildings in an army camp: one is a chapel, one a lecture room – a place for peace and a place for war-instruction. A difference in spirit begins to be noticeable. When the building has been used for generations – a church or torture chamber for instance – the feeling of this spirit is stronger. The place becomes imprinted by a spirit. However much it becomes a chrome and plastic city, who can visit Hiroshima without remembering?

As places build up their soul atmosphere to support a spirit of place, so too do rooms within one building: this room, for instance, or even part of room, is a hearth, the warm social heart of a *home,* not just the centre of a house.

Nowadays space is expensive to build. We design therefore in time and space; some rooms are multi-used. We think of time-space management. Indeed, sometimes I tell my clients that what they need is not more space but a different timetable. Most built spaces are empty more than they are in use, but we need to think first about the spirit of these places before we make any decisions about multi-use.

Some of these 'spirits of place' are resilient, allowing places to be used for many purposes. Others are more fragile. A cross-country run does not do so much harm to woodland and farmland but to a wild, empty, lonely mountain it leaves a long echo of *use*; not appreciation, but exploitation! Even amongst people who will not admit to anything spiritual in our surroundings, many recognise that the gambling machines cannot be satisfactorily moved into a meditation centre when it is not in use. In the same way, the protective tranquillity of a kindergarten is threatened when it is used for excitable debates about economic survival in the evenings.

Architecturally, what can we do to help nurture this spirit of place? Externally it is a matter of conversation between what already *is* and what we bring afresh with a *new idea* – an idea inspired out of the future, inspired from beyond the physical earth. Internally the *occu*pants will be bounded by fixed

physical restraints – walls, floor, ceiling. We need to bring in something enlivening, changing, renewing, something with a cosmic rather than just a human-usage rhythm; and that, of course, is natural light.

We tend to think of architecture as substance, but this substance is just the lifeless mineral vessel. Light is the life-giving element and both in quality and quantity it is absolutely central to our wellbeing. While light affects all aspects of mind and body, its effects are most pronounced upon the feelings. Just as warmth is related to activity and will (as you notice if you try to work in an overheated room) so light is related to the feeling realm, so much so that we often describe light in terms which we describe our own moods, like 'gloomy' or 'gentle', 'harsh' or 'warm'.

Inadequate light has been linked with depression and suicide statistics; however, we must not just think of light as a matter of physical quantity but as a life-bearing principle. We can enhance this life by how we texture, shape and colour the substance that frames and receives the light; for we cannot see light itself, only its meeting with substance. Some quite attractive materials drink up light, leaving a place gloomy even with bright windows; misplaced or shallow-set windows lacking tonal transition, harsh geometry and gloss reflection all tend in the same direction.

Light gives life to a room. There can be too much – window walled classrooms used to be the fashion – or too little. Rooms without natural light – here I think of the movement to classrooms with no windows at all – can have very disturbing effects upon physical, mental and social health. Laboratory rats in these circumstances attack each other or damage themselves. Some observers notice similar behaviour in those windowless schools.

The amount of window area we need to achieve particular lighting levels varies according to geography, orientation, climate and surrounding vegetation and topography as well as to the design of rooms and placing of windows. The amount of light we need likewise varies according to where we are in the world. City dwellers need more, so do those who live in northern latitudes or under predominantly grey skies, while towards the Mediterranean slatted shutters are used to darken rooms, creating quiet, cool sanctuaries from the outdoor heat.

It is easy to tell when there is not enough light in a room, when the windows are too small, but harder when they are too big. In Holland there are often a lot of plants and trees right outside the windows; the windows are big but the rooms gently lit. Candlelight gives life to a dark room which, poorly lit by a weak electric bulb, would be depressingly gloomy, and this is also the case with a sunbeam reflected off white-washed walls. To give life to a room it is much more a matter of quality than quantity. The human spirit needs this life-filled light. The soul needs it. Even the body needs it for physical health.

Nant-y-Cwm, Steiner Kindergarten

Sky-light from different directions and sunlight at different times of day have different qualities which breathe into our states of being throughout each day. Quantitatively west light may be the same as east. In quality they are distinctly different. The light of the seasons awakens us physically in the summer. In the winter its withdrawal awakens us to more inner activity.

Religious buildings – temples, cathedrals, stone circles – were built to correspond with chosen points in these great cosmic rhythms. Even today, simply for reasons of delight to the soul, we orientate windows to catch the sunrise early in the year and to be filled with water-reflected light at midsummer noon and direct, deeply penetrating sunbeams in the winter. We can work with reflection. It needs care, however; reflection from snow can warm a solar collector or lighten a dark room, but the light is cold and there can be dazzle and glare problems. Reflections from mirrors can cause problems of deceptive space. Some designers like to play with this, but being deceived does not strengthen a sense of roots. We can also use reflection from natural materials and from paint. As I have mentioned, the delicate breath of lazure colour gives more life to the light than heavy opaque paint which emphasises that static impenetrability of surfaces.

Once we think of reflection, we think of material and substance. The right materials make a building. In the days of black and white if I photographed an attractive village street the photograph would often show mediocre architecture. The colour, light effects of sunlight and materials, not to mention its unphotographable sensory richness, *made* the place.

Materials and light are two completely opposite poles which belong together. Thick walls with sunbeams through deep windows, dark rocks in luminously still water, trees fringed with light against the sun: these joy the heart. The unphotographable because they are alive. Light and matter is the greatest of architectural polarities – the polarity of cosmos and substance, one bringing enlivening, renewing rhythms, the other stable, enduring, rooted in place and time. This polarity is the foundation of health-giving architecture, for the oneness of stability, balance and renewal underlies health.

The ancient druids worked with this polarity with rock and sun, for in the tension between them health-giving life arises. I also try to work with it in a qualitative way, and it is sensitivity to qualities that has led me in this direction rather than thinking my way. I started just by having a *feeling* for these things. I have therefore made a lot of mistakes, but the process I have gone through is similar to that with which one needs to nurture a spirit of place.

It starts with developing a feeling for what is the appropriate mood, then building a strong soul of a place with materials and experiences of appropriate sensory qualities. It starts with the feelings; architecture built up out of adjectives – architecture for the soul.

Notes
1   This system, developed by PA Yeomans for Australian climatic conditions, has been widely and successfully used to reclaim and improve dryland prone to infrequent but destructively heavy rain.
2   Ell: fingertip to elbow measurement. It is particularly useful when laying stonework as a quick guide to the size of stones needed to complete a course.

(Extracts from Places of the Soul *by Christopher Day, Thorsons, London, March 1993)*

Organic Development of Place
In many people's minds, development in the countryside means its destruction – a view supported by the evidence of recent years. Nonetheless, pre-industrial development has given us a heritage of beautiful farmsteads, hamlets and villages. There *has* been a way for development to be harmonious.

Vernacular building (and life-style), however, resulted from unconscious habitual intuition, wise but unfree. Nowadays we have to consciously choose to act in harmony with nature and struggle to understand how to do so.

Not all growth in demand for buildings can reasonably be confined to reclaimed derelict land, urban infill and densification of existing settlements. As some inevitably must be accommodated in the countryside it is essential that a new way be found to foster harmony between buildings, human activities and countryside. At present, however, financial criteria, technological prowess and de-localised consciousness cause a disregard of the time, growth and life forces that have brought places into being, resulting in development unrelated to the reasons places have come to be the way they are, and buildings imposed without response to time or place.

There *are* ways of uniting buildings and surroundings so that they can belong together as inevitably as do those from the vernacular era. These involve organic growth processes, ecologically whole (and visible) life support cycles underpinned by (objectively) sensitive techniques of studying place and developing design proposals. Some of these I can describe.

Dr Colquhoun and I have been working with the following process as a group activity: we start by silent, non-judgmental listening to the place, through first impressions. Next we observe and record all the physical phenomena we can. We then attempt to understand how the place has been formed by the past and then extrapolate this into the future – how will it change if nothing is done? If there are minimal interventions (like changing the grazing regime, restricting vehicle speed)? If there are progressively more and major interventions (from cutting single trees to major abuse)?

Nant-y-Cwm, Steiner Kindergarten

Next we try to describe the responses invoked in us. Through this, the essential being of a place and what change it can or cannot accept can become clear.

The next stage is to work with the idea that is seeking to incarnate as a building. What is the essence of this idea? What activities does this generate? (The presence of an activity colours a whole area, even if it is invisible behind closed doors – have you ever been past a pilgrimage church or a nuclear power plant?) It is now possible to establish building edges with poles and string. These can be recorded onto scale drawings, modified to make more meaningful plans and then developed into three dimensions in clay. The next step is to introduce eye-level views of the clay model onto drawings or paintings of the place as it is. Through this process, that which was an idea needing to be rooted on earth, has become one with an evolving place in organic harmony. Instead of dominating imposition, the idea has made its first concrete step into *incarnation*.

Urban life is sustained by inputs of food, clean air, water, energy and materials; with pollution outputs (such as sewage, refuse etc). This life-support system is largely invisible, leading to a lack of consciousness with devastating consequences – it is at the root of the ecological crisis we are now entering. This model is increasingly duplicated even in the countryside where healthier systems are much easier to implement – indeed until a few decades ago they have been the norm. There is a strong case for requiring *all* new rural development to be largely self-sustaining and non-polluting in its life-support systems. As such systems need to be within daily consciousness, it is important that they are attractive.

Places have been formed by the past. Any change in the future is a development of the past – unless there is conscious human action. We now have the capacity to have ideas freed from habitual and geographical constraints. We can build anything anywhere. We frequently do, and it is frequently harshly out of place.

Modern development we can characterise as building to enclose future life-activities whereas vernacular development, inevitably harmonious, was building to consolidate growing life-activities. It was underpinned by two principles – growth from life-nodes and organic development. Principles no less essential today.

Modern growth nodes are often existing settlements but they include such unromantic places as bus stops and car parks – places where informal activities from bottle-banks to ice-cream vans spring up. Usually there is something already there but some agricultural, research and educational activities may develop where no obvious node previously existed. Growth nodes must be life-filled meeting points. They depend upon life – human social and economic life or life in nature. This is always richest at the meeting of different qualities of landscape – woodland edge, waterside, pasture-arable boundary and so on. Typically, vernacular settlements grew from such meeting points.

A vital key to successful new development is identifying meaningful growth nodes. Next comes development by strategy rather than masterplan. Here we can seek to build every stage to create a *perfect* present, yet allow scope for new paths and nodes, along with infill, densification and intensification of use, so that the future can be *even better*. This is how our ancestors built, unconsciously. We can do it consciously.

I have described techniques for the right placing of buildings and their related activities. The rightness of placing can be further strengthened if we use sensory 'markers' such as turns in path, tree archways etc, to strengthen approach experience so that buildings become the inevitable conclusion of an experiential journey. However, to really belong, as it were, inevitably in place, they also need appropriate qualities, particularly of scale, form, colour and materials, and linking elements.

In a landscape setting, building scale needs to be as small as possible. Also, using low buildings utilising roof space, siting in hollows and against backdrops, and building into slopes can help. Buildings need to be significantly smaller than trees and these vary significantly according to geographical factors. Hardness and brightness of colour have a marked effect on visual impact; think of the same building, soft-edged in natural local stone, lime-washed, or smooth rendered and sharp edged painted with masonry paint. In general, the brighter the colour, harder the texture or larger the scale, the other qualities need to be quieter, softer and smaller. Subject to not looking out of place with the neighbouring built language, curved forms, vegetated walls and earth colours and local materials tend to blend in harmoniously.

Not to appear temporarily parked, buildings need to be 'rooted' in the ground – traditionally by flaring or stepped bases, though ground be used to tie buildings into place – as is easily demonstrated by drawing them onto a picture of any building disharmoniously placed in its surroundings.

We cannot satisfactorily imitate, but can learn from the past, and translate this into modern forms of understanding, planning, design and landscaping. These are based on three principles: firstly, marriage of past (place) and future (idea), secondly, ecological and aesthetic harmony and mutual responsiveness and, thirdly, organic development from life-activity growth nodes.

In the limited instances where building development is appropriate in the countryside, this approach can foster wholeness, harmony and health of place. It can also be a model for suburban and urban development to heal the wounds already built. *(Chapter taken from the draft of* Beyond Green, *Christopher Day)*

Nant-y-Cwm, Steiner Kindergarten

GREG LYNN
MULTIPLICITOUS AND IN-ORGANIC BODIES

Types of Spatial Bodies
It is obvious, moreover, that mathematical organisation imposed on stone is none other than the completion of an evolution of earthly forms, whose meaning is given, in the biological order, by the passage of the simian to the human form, the latter already presenting all the elements of architecture. In morphological progress men apparently represent only an intermediate stage between monkeys and great edifices. Forms have become more and more static, more and more dominant. The human order from the beginning is, just as easily, bound up with architectural order, which is no more than its development. *Georges Bataille*

In 1949, Rudolf Wittkower systematised a theory of harmonic proportion by uncovering a single spatial type in the domestic architecture of Andrea Palladio. Indeed, he discovered Palladio, one might say, by inventing an origin for his work. Wittkower's theory continues to provide a general rule for the definition of essential architectural structure: the nine-square grid. The exact geometry of this type guarantees its universal applicability. In *The Origin of Geometry* of 1936, Edmund Husserl establishes exact geometries through a kind of phenomenological reduction that eliminates differences through 'variations'. Similarly, Wittkower exploits the differences between eleven of Palladio's villas for their ability to cancel each other out. For the cancellation of disparate elements manifests a 'hidden' typological order: through a 'return inquiry' the nine-square grid emerges as the universal origin of each of the villas. For Wittkower, the type is not merely a constellation of mathematical correspondences, but further, a system of spatial organisation that functions as a unified and self-regulating body. The nine-square grid, through harmonic proportion, makes each villa in particular, and the twelve villas in general, whole. Two years earlier, in *The Mathematics of the Ideal Villa*, Colin Rowe used the same nine-square grid type to crossbreed two pairs of twins: Le Corbusier's Villa Savoye with Palladio's Villa Rotonda, and Le Corbusier's Villa Stein with Andrea Palladio's Villa Malcontenta. Both 'progeny' seem less than natural kin to the villas (the type relying on variations between villas and never fully present in any villa in particular but present in all villas in general). It is, nevertheless, the proportional correspondence of these often contradictory spatial organisations that lays the groundwork for a single cubic spatiality from which a *whole species* of villas were born. For Rowe, the proportional harmony of the spatial body of the nine-square grid hidden within all ideal villas evoked a 'Virgilian tranquility'.

Rather than continue this logic of burial and recovery of origins for architecture, might there be another way to respect particularities and differences without 'returning our inquiry' to universal types? Today we confront a different but related problem: What is the nature of the interior of architecture? What lies hidden within this interior? These questions are already thematised within architecture through the erection of boundaries that establish the difference, and degree of autonomy, between the inside and outside. Yet before determining where to begin with architectural interiority – which is a problem of finding an entry – we have to question the origin of the interior. In the work of Vitruvius we find the first clue as to the problem of the type and content of this interior space. He identified an internal 'proportional balance which results from principles of symmetry in architecture'. Vitruvius expressed remorse that, like a living body, the breast of architecture could never be opened to reveal the secrets of its interior. The architectural orders of proportion and symmetry are not simply already present within architecture; according to Vitruvius, they have been intentionally concealed so that questions of interiority can be posed only within a closed harmonic system. This geometric system of proportion, as Wittkower, Rowe and Vitruvius have argued, is itself a whole. This description of architecture as a harmonic, naturally proportioned organism is indebted to the operation of two 'purloined secrets' within an inviolate interior: geometry and the body.

Unity of the Organism and the Eidetic Language of Geometry
The design of a temple depends on symmetry, the principles of which must be most carefully observed by the architect. They are due to proportion, in Greek. Proportion is a correspondence among the measures of the members of an entire work, and of the whole to a certain part selected as standard. From this result the principles of symmetry. Without symmetry and proportion there can be no principles in the design of any temple; that is, if there is no precise relation

between its members, as in the case of those of a well shaped man. *Vitruvius*

Pure geometry and kinematics (and all the associated sciences for which they are the example here), then, will be material eidetics, since their purpose is the thingly, and thus the corporeal, determination of objects in general. But they are abstract material sciences, because they only treat certain eidetic components of corporeal things in general, disregarding their independent and concrete totality, which also comprises the 'material' (stofflich), sensible qualities and the totality of their predicates. Spatial shapes, temporal shapes, and shapes of motion are always singled out from the totality of the perceived body. By itself alone, then, a static analysis could a priori and rigorously recall for us that the protogeometer always already had at his disposal anexact spatiotemporal shapes and essentially 'vague' morphological types, which can always give rise to a pre-geometrical descriptive science. This could be called geography. For such a subject, the rigour of eidetic assertions (like that for determining vague essences) is not at all undermined by the necessary anexactitude of the perceived object. We must indeed beware of scientific naivete, which causes this anexactitude of the object or concept to be considered as a 'defect,' as an inexactitude. *Jacques Derrida*

In architecture, structure is drawn within things. As Bataille has suggested, architecture is the locale where the universality of geometry binds the base matter of temporal bodies. The regulating lines of architectural orders make a connection to the world as a whole, but also to the specific morphological characteristics of forms. Spatial types are involved in the practice of originating families of form (as in the constitution of 'species' such as Wittkower's brood of villas). Architectural types organise amorphous matter. Architectural proportion, moreover, achieves the transcendental status of an abstract, holistic and organic body. It adopts the logic of an organism, which is above and beyond either mathematics or matter. What distinguishes harmonic proportion from mathematical measure is the value granted to specific ratios based on the symmetrical unity of all parts to a whole. The terms *organic, organism* and *organisation* can be used interchangeably to the extent that they all delimit things which are *whole* – that is, containing both a rigid external boundary, 'to which nothing can be added or subtracted without jeopardising the balance of the composition', and an interior space closed to the unpredicted and contingent influences of external forces. It is important to qualify these ideal bodies as whole to the fullest extent, complete to the point of exclusion. This organic logic of proportion is already embedded within architecture's interior.

Architecture's provision for structure, use and shelter necessitates an absolute and exact delimitation of internal volume from external forces. To signify this rigid sense of the interior, architecture frequently invokes the paradigm of the inviolate interior of a living body. Le Corbusier's Modular provides an obvious example of the alignment of the body with measure. Of course, the paradigmatic body is both docile and static; its particularities of culture, history, race, development and degeneration are repressed in favour of a general model. Even the Husserlian notion of 'variation' places the particular in the service of the average or mean. The typology of natural orders is always underwritten by the variable measurement of difference between and within species. For instance, the evolutionary transformation 'From Frog to Apollo,' which appeared in the 1803 edition of Johann Casper Lavater's *Physiognomische Fragmente*, exploited both the constellation of particularities and differences between the frog and the ideal man and a continuous and general *faciality* that registers these differences.

Rather than reducing the differential variations between elements to an invariant static type, Lavater employs a continuous, differentiated system of transformation. A similar method of Cartesian deformation was developed in 1917 by the morphologist D'Arcy Thompson to describe the transformations of natural form in response to environmental forces. Thompson provisionally aligned bodies and measure in such a way that particular dissymmetries and disproportions were maintained as events within a deformable, supple, non-eidetic and irreducible geometric system of description. Geometry becomes not a static measure of invariant and unitary characteristics but what Deleuze and Guattari have referred to as a 'plane of consistency' upon which differential transformations and deformations occur. Type itself is never present in a fixed state in an entire species. Thus a more fluid and dynamic system of measure can be employed to describe ever-changing spatial bodies through their manifestations at singular moments. In Thompson's deformations, particular information influences and transforms a general grid, making geometry more compliant to the matter it describes. The enlargement of a fish's eye is registered in the deformation of its accompanying grid. The dimensional fluctuation became, for Thompson, an indication of light level and water depth influencing that particular species. In this manner, the type or spatial organism is no longer seen as a static whole separate from external forces, but rather as a sensibility continuously transforming through its internalisation of outside events. But within the pact of the organism and the geometric language with which it is exactly described, these fluid characteristics are generally reduced to fixed principles.

To understand this better we must look to the language of geometry with an eye towards those moments where it describes spaces and forms as whole bodies. It is in fact most likely not utility, economy or structure that fixes architecture statically, but its prejudice in favour of geometric idealism. Geometry provides the apparently universal language with which architecture assumes to speak through history, across culture and over time. Architecture tends to employ geometries that are eidetic: that it is, they are manifest visually as pure spatial coordinates; they are self-identical, signifying nothing other than themselves; they are repeatable identically; and they are absolutely translatable for all people for all time. For example, geometry need posit only one 'sphere' as a surface composed of an infinite number of points equidistant from a single radius. In effect, the sphere that existed for Plato has been handed down to us identically across cultures and through history. 'Vague' objects that are merely round may be more or less spherical yet no two are ever absolutely identical. 'Roundness' itself can be defined with probability but never ideally described with exactitude. Likewise, an ideal sphere can never be realised in matter. Certain things are believed to be spherical even though their specific matter guarantees that they can never achieve pure form. Vague forms that do not repress the particular characteristics of matter are typically considered to be inexact. Geometric exactitude, in other words, tends to transform particularities, no matter how precise they may be, into inexactitudes through mathematical reduction. It renders particularities and difference as mere variations beneath which subsists a more fixed and universal language of proportions.

Proportional bodies are bound by geometric exactitude: These ideal spatial organisms are reducible and identically repeatable. They have the appeal of being stated 'once and for all'. In systems of proportion, architecture assumes a natural relationship between geometry, with its claims to exact measure, and the unified stasis of an organism, with its claims to wholeness. Because of its predilection for fixity and stasis, architecture has become the privileged site for the elision of eidetic geometry and holistic organisation. Yet we should beware of any architecture described as wholesome or organic, for the logic of the organism is the logic of self-enclosure, self-regulation and self-determination. Organic types that are whole to the fullest extent are full to the point of exclusion. Buildings are not organisms but merely 'organs', provisional structures, that are already multiplicitous. Where the organic is internally consistent, the 'inorganic' is internally discontinuous and capable of a multiplicity of unforeseen connections. To disentangle the pact between organic bodies and exact geometric language that underlies architecture's static spatial types is a monumental task. Any attempt to loosen this alliance must simultaneously 'de-territorialise' the autonomy of whole organisms and replace the exactitude of rigid geometry with more pliant systems of description.

Like all forms of writing, architecture is neither exact nor inexact but 'anexact'. A more supple geometric description of architectural form would necessarily loosen the connection to organic models of proportional harmony and stasis through a flexible compliance to particularities. For example, Thompson's deformations subject the stasis of geometric types to dynamic transformation through the internalisation of particular, vague or anexact characteristics. With a less whole and wholesome paradigm of the body, not only do typologies become dispersed, but moreover, their interiors open to productive alliances. That is to say, spatial bodies other than the ideal types are brought into affiliations with systems outside of their boundaries, where their determinacy at any point in time is dependent upon influence by external events. Gilles Deleuze and Felix Guattari have proposed such a model for a 'body without organisation': the organic, bound by a unified and internally consistent model of the organism, is reformulated as a multiplicity of affiliated organs without any single reductive organisation. In architecture, the present static alliance between rigid geometry and whole organisms cannot be entirely overcome but may be made more flexible and fluid through the use of more supple or deformable geometry.

Geometry resists the play of writing more than any other language. Bataille's idea of the *informe,* or 'formless', recognises the capacity to both define and defer form within a practice of writing. This 'informal' practice writes the anomalies in a manner that is amorphous. Denis Hollier, writing through Bataille in *Against Architecture,* implies that the *informe* of writing can only be arrested *in form* by architecture. But rather than locating the refusal of form solely within philosophy, the formless might also be written within architecture by architects. The most transgressive moment of Bataille's *informe* occurs where the formless is found to be already within the *'mathematical frock coat'* of form. Informal writing within architecture leads, as previously suggested, towards a different kind of alliance between geometry and the organism, resulting in anexact, multiplicitous, temporal, supple, fluid, disproportionate and monstrous spatial bodies. Unlike exact geometry, informal writing accommodates differences in matter by resisting any reductions to ideal form. Because of this hesitation to arrest forms once and for all, their descriptions become more compliant to the base matter they signify.

Monumentality and Multiplicity

The other type of multiplicity appears in pure duration: it is an internal multiplicity of succession, of fusion, of organisation, of heterogeneity, of qualitative discrimination, or of *difference in kind*; it is a *virtual and continuous* multiplicity that cannot be reduced to numbers. *Gilles Deleuze* Architecture reserves its strongest statements for monuments. The monument commemorates an event that is experienced through shared (particularly urban) histories by offering a unitary and repeatable space. Therefore it is in the monument that the allegiance between exact geometries and organic models of the body are strongest. Hollier incriminates architecture for its monumental mode of discourse. He executes this judgement through a critical strategy similar to that which Derrida employed in his introduction to Husserl's *Origin of Geometry,* arguing that architecture's 'origin is still lacking at the beginning'. It is the idea, again, that architecture unifies itself by continually originating ideal spatial bodies that can only be invoked after the fact of their variations. In monuments, architecture 'arrests' events in form by defining ideal urban spatial bodies in exact geometric terms. Bataille's and Hollier's rejection of architecture as a potential practice of writing depends on the assumption that proportional order originates in and is natural to architecture. In this scenario, the privileging of monumentality precludes any description of form other than by arrest. The challenge to architecture, once geometry and the body enter into a new alliance, is to write – in form – a monument that is irreducible to any ideal geometric type. To refuse the transcendence of static form, architecture must begin to describe the particular characteristics of incompletion rejected by the exactitude of geometry and the symmetry of proportion.

Deleuze and Guattari's aforementioned 'body without organs' suggests an alternative to the organic paradigm of the whole body. Such a multiplicitous body is always less than a single organism at the same time that it is an affiliation of many organs. Deleuze and Guattari extension of Elias Canetti's paradigm of the pack, swarm or crowd is one model for engaging a less-than-whole building within a context that is an assemblage of often disparate morphologies rather than a continuous fabric. The behaviour of the pack does not turn on the distinctions between part and whole, autonomous individual and collective. To become intensively involved with such an organisation, an individual must enter into the affiliative alliances of the pack. There is a two-fold de-territorialisation that takes place in becoming a multiplicity: the loss of internal boundaries allows both the influence of external events within the organism and the expansion of the interior outward. This generates a body that is essentially inorganic. For instance, within a multiplicitous assemblage, each individual defers their internal structure to benefit, by alliance, from the fluid movements of the pack. As the proper limits of individual elements (multiplicity of, say, wolves) are blurred, the pack begins to behave as if it were itself an organism (multiplicity of the pack). The pack itself is not regulated by or reducible to any single structure, as it is continually, dynamically and fluidly transforming itself in response to its intensive involvement with both the external forces of its

context and the internal forces of its members. Multiplicity describes both the assembly of a provisional group from disparate elements – which is less than a whole – and the already less-than-whole nature of each of those elements that are allied with the group. Multiplicitous bodies are always already entering into relations and alliances through multiple *plications*. Structures such as these are not identically repeatable outside of the particularities of their internal elements or their external environments. In architecture, the multiplicitous connections of buildings to the particularities of context are typically repressed by the proportion of exact, unified, organic spatial types. One example that speaks to structural issues of multiplicity is the planarian or flatworm. Within the body of a single planarian is a very specific constellation of possibilities for the proliferation of a multiplicity of bodies. The limits of this development is determined both by the internal structure of the animal and by the lines of development imposed from outside its body. The developments that result along these lines can only be described by their affiliations.

Affiliative Connections and the Colossus

We still have something in common to them all; and using another mathematical term (somewhat loosely perhaps) we may speak of the *discriminant characters* which persist unchanged, and continue to form the subject of our transformation. But the method, far as it goes, has its limitations. We cannot fit both beetle and cuttlefish into the same framework, however we distort it; nor by any co-ordinate transformation can we turn either of them into one another or into the vertebrate type. They are essentially different; there is nothing about them which can be legitimately compared. *D'Arcy Thompson*

A unique plane of consistency or composition for the cephalopod and the vertebrate; for the vertebrate to become an Octopus or Cuttlefish, all it would have to do is fold itself . . . *Plication.* It is no longer a question of organs and functions, and of a transcendent Plane that can preside over their organisation only by means of analogical relations and types of divergent development. *Gilles Deleuze*

There is in the colossal an attraction, a particular charm, to which the theories of ordinary art are hardly applicable. *Fredric Auguste Bartholdi*

If, 'originally, the word [kolossos] has no implication of size', it will come to have this implication later only *by accident.* What about this accident, this one *in particular*, which brings cise to the colossus, not the incisive cise which gives measure, not the moderating [moderate rice] cise but the *disproportionate* [demesurante] cise? *Jacques Derrida*

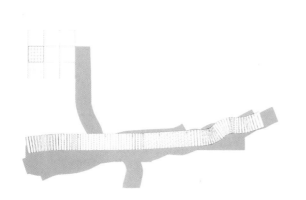
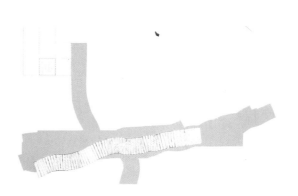

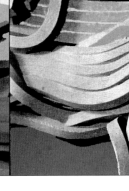

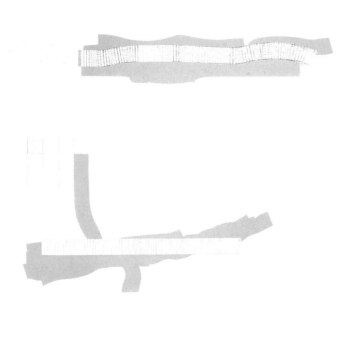
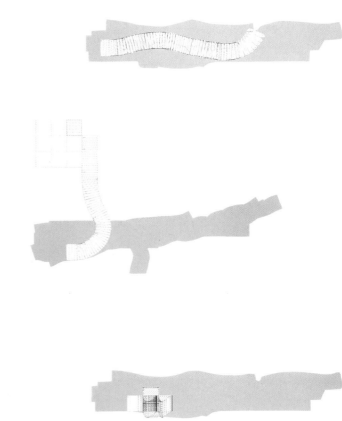

The Sears Tower: Plan, sections and views of model

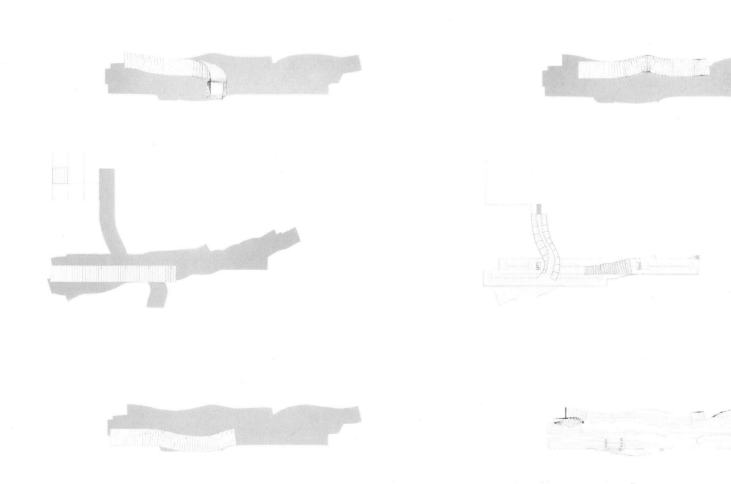

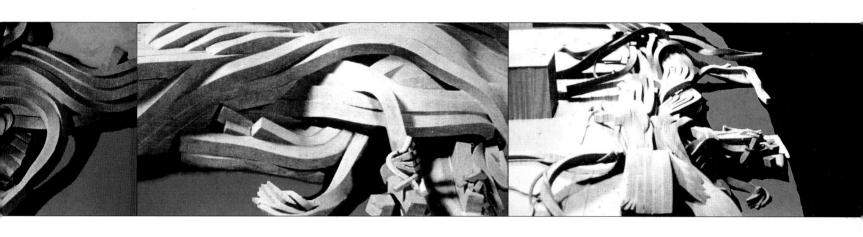

I use the word *affiliative* to describe a system of connections characteristic of a multiplicitous organism against the idea of the filiative. The latter implies the relations of a family, of proper parents and progeny. But the proper family values established through such an evolution often overlook the alliances of different species that develop along lines of *involution*. The distinction between the two strategies is aptly illustrated by the debate between D'Arcy Thompson, who favours essential unchanging species, and Gilles Deleuze, who folds these species into each other. Thompson situates essential differences on a fixed geometric plane of comparison (similar to the faciality of Lavater's transformations). Deleuze attacks the essentialism of difference between these species by rendering this plane as a complex of folded connections between disparate species.

Categories of form, such as the idea of 'species distinction,' provide for a return to an original type from which subsequent spatial organisations develop. These types are reinvented each time they are invoked. Any evolutionary discourse that employs straight filial lines of development and pyramidal hierarchies of species is founded on the relations between families of forms. And these filial relations are weighted in favour of general principles. The prejudice toward fixed orders is achieved at the cost of repressing local differences of programme, structure, form and culture. Affiliative relations, by contrast, typically exploit possible connections that occur through vicissitude. They cannot be predicted by the global systems of organisation present in any single unified organism. When *whole* systems of geometric description and organisation break down, seemingly unnatural connections between disparate elements emerge. The introduction into architecture of forms that are 'protogeometric', or without exact measure, presents such an opportunity.

Robert Venturi's paradigmatic *'duck'* is a possible multiplicitous body. The *duck* is founded on sculptural, not-yet-architectural figures, generally considered to be in conflict with structural and pragmatic requirements. The assumed natural contradiction of the pragmatic by the figural denies any possibility for a complicitous relationship between decoration and structure. Colossal statuary invites characterisation as ducks: sculptures-becoming-buildings. The scale of colossal statuary requires architectural design; yet the complex negotiations among figure, structure, and programme are repressed in favour of an iconic and singular sculptural form. In the Statue of Liberty, the enlargement of the one-to-one scale of the human figure to the monumental scale of the city meant that its sculptor, Frederic Auguste Bartholdi, had to collaborate with Viollet-le-Duc and, later, Gustaf Eiffel. This collaboration, however, was not familial but unpredicted. The enlargement, 'beyond theories of art,' introduced an anomalous form that was neither sized nor 'incised' before its entry into architecture.

The introduction of this particular amorphous figure, the Statue of Liberty, which did not originate in architecture, provokes new connections with the conventions of drawing, measurement, construction, use and context. By beginning with bodies of disproportionate matter rather than with spatial types a more supple affiliation ensues between geometry and the 'thing' described. No single proper filial line ever exists between amorphous or base matter and the mathematics of form. The description of these anexact morphological types can be precise yet will inevitably require empirical methods that are compliant to the matter with which they begin. Both Venturi's duck and the colossus, through size, introduce an alien form prior to the origination of an organic geometric system of proportion. This differs entirely from a more familiar anthropomorphism wherein the body forms a link between nature and architecture through geometric proportional correspondences of part to whole, microcosm to macrocosm. Colossal architecture instead introduces a disproportionate body that both precedes and resists geometric exactitude. Despite its singularity as a sculptural object, the Statue of Liberty's multiplicitous assembly of contingent and compliant substructures results from an internal resistance to any single proper form or type. Further, the compliancy between the designs of Bartholdi and Eiffel engenders unforeseen affiliations among pylons, trusses, tertiary grids, substructures, skins, ornaments, and their various interconnections without appealing to contradiction. Rather, it joins figural and structural systems symbiotically. The effects of the colossal scale, then, are visible not only in the enlargement of the singular body but, more importantly, in the unpredicted local relationships of disparate building systems.

There is more than a dialectic relationship operating between Bartholdi and Eiffel. Although Bartholdi provided the original sculptural form that Eiffel was employed to structure, the work of each was altered in the bargain. The result of their combination is measured not by mere addition but by multiplication. On close examination, Liberty's body is found to be riddled with gridded fissures. It is the site of a general topological gridding that flexibly coordinates the particularities of the specific folds of the body and fabric that drape it. The rigid geometry of the hidden structural pylon infects the folded surface with a system of lines that seems arbitrary in this particular body. Simultaneously, the pure structure of Eiffel's pylon has been deflected to one side to accommodate the nonsymmetrical posture of a woman with a raised arm. In contrast to the Eiffel Tower, the specific posture of the Statue of Liberty lacks general symmetry. The particularities of Liberty's gestures across its surface cause differential torsional adjustments that proliferate locally throughout the steel structure.

Although less obvious in its boldness, the connection of the pylon to the skin of the statue was at least equally inventive. From the massive central tower a secondary system of lightweight trusswork reaches out on all sides toward the interior surface of the figure . . . Points of attachment are provided on the copper skin itself by an inner webbing of strapwork which acts to consolidate the thin member as well. This secondary trusswork is joined to the webbed skin not by rigid connections, but by what amounts to a tertiary level of structure . . . The skin, in other words, is not rigidly attached to the armature, but floats at the ends of hundreds of flexible members that form a suspension to which the entire skin adheres. Floating thus on springs, the thin copper envelope is given an extraordinary *supple* elasticity.   *Marvin Trachtenberg*

More significant than either the figural influences on the grid or the gridding of the figure is the development of fortuitous, contingent subsystems between these two. The secondary network of connections between the trusswork and the inner surface – an inner webbing of thousands of flexible members – exists only because of the affiliation between these disparate systems. The elements that negotiate between the trusses and the draped body could not be predicted within either the architectural or the sculptural discourse. There is a colossal disproportion of these parts to the whole. Neither the architectural nor the sculptural origin of the building can dominate the symbiotic network of affiliated subsystems that construct the seemingly singular iconic figure of the colossus.

Thus the alliance between Bartholdi and Eiffel produces not a singular organism but a multiplicity of organs. In the architectural drawings, or incisings, of the colossus, the iconic structure of the statue is diffused. Each specific cutting plane is oblique to the figure of the particular body since there is no single plane on which to projected its form. The colossus is irreducible to any single measure or geometric description – apart from its size; for a multiplicitous body is generated from an interaction of internal logics with external events. Nevertheless, when comparing the plans, we find that a nine-square grid more or less spans from the central pylon to the skin. Yet the nine-square bay system introduced by the structural tower varies in response to the contours of the folded skin. Eiffel's structure is a provisional structure, then, rather than an essential organisational type like the nine-square of Rowe and Wittkower.

This resistance of amorphous matter to incisement or reduction to proportional measure is characteristic of the colossus. Unlike sculpture, the discipline of architecture is founded on the drawing of a thing before its existence. It is the secondary, or what Robin Evans refers to as the *alterior*, status of architectural description that is resisted in the Liberty's plans and sections. Its geometric co-ordinates come after, and are thus compliant to, the thing they describe. The geometries that incise the colossal are therefore pliant and supple. The colossus is a body that cannot be reduced to its original size or simplicity, a body that resists the proportional co-ordination of an anthropomorphic organism. In the Statue of Liberty the architectural quality (other than firmness or structure) that distinguishes the colossus from sculpture is an aleatory commodiousness within the interior. The occupation of the folds of the dress, the blades of the crown, the strands of the hair, the muscular contours of the outstretched arm, and the profiles of the lips, nose, eyes, ears, chin and forehead, is neither accidental nor anthropomorphic, but results from unpredicted affiliations between a network of disparate subsystems that make contingent connections between a multiplicity of spaces.

PHIL HAWES
ECOLOGICALLY DESIGNED SYSTEMS
Architecture and Planning

Since the completion of the architectural work on the Biosphere 2 Project in Arizona last year, my office has been involved in the research and planning for the creation of a truly ecological community which would include a marketing facility.

The community, we call EcoVille, has, as one major component of its functional basis, the processes of living microbial systems which are responsible for the purification of the air and water of our planet. These processes are easily adapted to assist in the cleanup of what we usually call pollution or waste. 'Waste' can also be viewed as a resource which is located in the wrong place, at the wrong time, and in the wrong concentration.

The majority of ecological pollution problems facing the world today are solvable by known biotechnological means or by the substitution of less polluting methods of production. We now seem to be in a position to actually complete the industrial revolution, which has given us so much material progress, by completing the final phase of the manufacturing process, the cleanup. Any true craftsman is admired for keeping his tools correctly sharpened and for cleaning up the mess produced by his creative work. It is also considered a part of growing up to a responsible adulthood to hang up your clothes, bathe periodically, and in general keep your household in order. It is at this level of transition that we find ourselves; a need for growing maturity with respect to our waste products and their recycling.

It is now necessary for us to pay particular attention to the cleanup of our industry. Without this, our famous industrial revolution will very likely poison us and bring about the downfall of our world wide technological civilisation. Furthermore, it is neither desirable, nor is it possible, to return to nature as our aboriginal ancestors lived life. We are too numerous, and have lost the skills required for hunting and gathering as a way of existence.

Humanity must now evolve into a new relationship of symbiosis with nature based on a deeper understanding combined with an acceptance of our responsibility to become good stewards or managers of the planet's resources.

One definition of ecology is that it is the 'rules of the house'. Our planetary house must be kept in order by reducing waste, which is really misplaced resources, and by recycling intelligently. The planet itself does this admirably when not over-impacted by human behaviour.

The town that our office is designing elaborates upon and extends the idea of including educational facilites, to demonstrate to the public what 'green' can really mean, and applies it to the entire human habitat. Its basic form is adapted from studies we have conducted on the traditional villages of Provence in Southern France, and elsewhere, and the high level of success which is evident by their continued viability as functional and enjoyable habitations capable of satisfying changing human requirements, in many cases for over 2,000 years.

The basic form and ambience of these communities is adaptable to different cultural populations and situations. In addition to a community for 25,000 persons on 2,400 hectares we are working on a smaller proof-of-concept module (called Hilltop) which is a mini-community, or neighbourhood, of only five hectares. Both of these plans use certain basic principles of planning and design.

It has become increasingly evident that one of the major influences imposed by humanity and its urban aggregations on the total ecology of Earth is that of nutrient relocation. Plants and animals grown in rural areas are harvested and shipped to urban areas, often located in other countries or continents from their place of origin. This relocation creates huge concentrations of nutrients in the form of sewage and garbage, and deprives the rural areas of the recycling of that nutrient. In turn, this not only requires the application of imported chemical fertiliser to the farmyards, but more importantly, also creates situations where the nutrient-rich sewage is seen as waste to be disposed of as easily as possible by dumping it into rivers or the sea. Garbage is often buried in land fills or burned, and its nutrient value is lost.

Feed lots for cattle and pigs also build up large quantities of manure, which are considered uneconomical to ship to areas where it would be prized as fertiliser. Rainwater leaches the manure nutrients into the ground water causing serious nitrogen pollution problems in parts of Brittany, the US and elsewhere.

We have designed EcoVille as a group of urban nodes or clusters with greenhouse complexes and agricultural lands often penetrating to within 500 metres of the community cores to allow for controlled nutrient recycling. This allows the farmers access to the benefits of the urban living, cuts produce transportation costs, gives the urban dweller access to the countryside and generally

OPPOSITE: MarSphere, Mars atmospheric simulation test chamber and scientific support village

promotes an increased understanding of natural cycles and processes by which food is produced, and a greater understanding of the symbiosis between the urban and agricultural facets of the community.

Another result of the urban/rural design proximity that becomes quite apparent to the farmer and urbanite alike is the necessity of promoting integrated pest management and crop rotation as opposed to simply blanketing the total urban and rural community with toxic insecticides.

Transportation and communications must be of the highest quality to create a community in which it is easy to do business and to live well. It must be convenient to shop, and to access business and entertainment, and to enjoy life in general in a primarily pedestrian-centred community.

Critical to the urban fabric is the means of circulation and transport. Even in areas like Arizona where land is inexpensive $1,500 per acre it makes good sense to condense urban development into relatively dense pedestrian oriented clusters around light rail, monorail and other public transport stations. Therefore, we have designed EcoVille using a combination of the form of the Paris Metro and bus network and the relatively high population densities of the villages of Provence for liveability and ease of pedestrian access.

No private automobiles or other motor vehicles are allowed within the urban matrix of EcoVille with the exception of some small specialised electric vehicles for the handicapped and infirm. This is strictly enforced and results in the subsequent reduction of street widths and eliminates the need for parking buildings and lots. This basic infrastructure pattern reduces development costs to approximately 25 to 30 per cent of the typical American suburb with its characteristic sprawling form.

The latest in cutting-edge communications technology is used including a community fibre optic network, satellite up-link, multiple data base access and special arrangements for video phone and conferencing capabilities.

One of the most insidious aspects of town planning has been the practice of strict separation of residential, commercial, office, and manufacturing zones in modern town planning. This in turn has created functional ghettos of each of these zones of differentiated use, requiring extensive travel time between home and work. One of the keys to the future advance and evolution of humanity, and of Earth, is the absolute necessity to clean up industrial by-products. Mixing land uses so that residential, commercial, office, and manufacturing functions can coexist satisfactorily depends on eliminating the sources of pollution. This pollution is all non-life enhancing by-products of human creative production whether noise, dust, vapours, odour, vibrations, excess light, heat or trash.

Whether one is designing a green super market or a green community, the public educational compo-nent is paramount. There have been several note-worthy excursions into revealing the wonders of the ordinary to the tourist. Biosphere 2 is one such experiment. It is a privately financed effort to create a huge scientific apparatus built in such a way as to allow the public a high degree of access to the facility in order to view its workings as much as possible. Thus, the visitor can gain an understanding of the role that such biospheres can play by being separate environments apart from our everyday biosphere, Biosphere 1. With respect to data gathering, and as general investigative tools for increased ecological understanding of our planet, such facilities are uniquely valuable.

Modern merchandisers have mastered marketing to the point that people will buy that which they neither need, nor want, nor can properly digest. This has given rise to the concept of the 'consumer'. A more appropriate idea is the old fashioned one of 'customer'. A consumer is defined as, 'One who uses up, devours, expends or destroys by use'; it also means, 'That which causes to waste away'. Customer is a more ecological word, defined as, 'A buyer, a patron'. Customer relates to consumer, as gourmet, or epicure, relates to glutton. The physical architecture of a market needs to create an ambience not of frantic and compulsive consuming, but one of reasoned choice.

There have been some outstanding steps taken in this direction such as the listing of the ingredients of packaged goods, labelling of weights and prices per gram. For example, a container of yoghurt weighing a pound (500 grams) is shown as costing so many cents per net ounce. Then, regardless of package weight the consumer can compare products.

The green super market can demonstrate how life and life processes are responsible for the cleansing of Earth's air and water through the use of plant microbial soil/air purification reactors. These apparatuses circulate contaminated air through soil-plant combination assemblies to remove carbon monoxide, methane, etc. Waste water is also channelled through landscaped eco-garden march systems to withdraw nutrients, destroy pathogenic bacteria, transmute organic chemicals to CO_2 and water vapour, and extract heavy metals.

The urbanite throughout the world is cut off from the food production process. 'Where is my food from, how is it fertilised, harvested, processed? What is added to it and what is taken away from the natural food? How does this effect me and my family? Is the soil where my children's food is grown depleted of vital trace elements? What can be done to supplement that? Is the honey contaminated by radioactivity?' These are some of the questions that a genuinely responsible entrepreneur will need to investigate in the very near future and then pass the answer on to the buyer, if he expects to truly serve his customers and keep their business.

Most markets of today don't concern themselves with these questions. Assuming that the current interest in our planet's ecology and our own well-being is not simply some fad or aberration, but comes from an intelligently directed need to know, the consideration of the questions above will shape the markets and the agriculture of the immediate future.

It is too much to expect that our governments will take care of everything for us. Research into the truths of nature and humanities' impact upon it is not a divinely mandated duty of the state. Customers' interest is now driving the producers and marketing establishments to investigate and reveal just what they are selling. The developing 'green consciousness' will soon want to be convinced as to the correctness of the crops fed to the animals that are in turn fed to us. Animal hormones and growth stimulators now used need further critical research to determine their effects, as do a broad variety of food preservatives.

Mistakes have been made and will continue to be made, but now we are conscious of some of the dangers of our own creativeness and cleverness and are therefore forewarned to examine. We cannot, of course, ever know everything. Only recently have research scientists become aware of some of the effects of man-made and natural organic compounds and their dangers as well as their benefits. No longer do pesticide salesmen peddle their wares by eating a spoonful of DDT to prove to the farmer that, 'It only kills insects and is harmless to people'. The world is more sophisticated and we are aware that we have been burned through our own ignorance.

A truly 'super' market entrepreneur must be concerned with the real quality of his products far beyond their outward appearance. He will not only not take advantage of buyers in their ignorance, but will also seek to develop his own understanding of the totality of his merchandise, its origin, processing, and ingredients, and then go out of his way to pass on this understanding to the customer.

Some scientists maintain that we are now in an era that necessitates the management of all levels of Earth's natural resources from the atomic and electromagnetic to the ecology of entire rivers' drainage basins and even continents. It is necessary to make this an era of increased intelligent inquiry and research in order to determine what correct management means. This is the ecological approach, the world view of total life systems orientation and the striving for holistic understanding.

The world of life is very powerful in its ability to cleanse our environment, but still very mysterious in many of its methods.

Something seemingly as simple as demonstrating ecological principles in a super market complex can have far reaching effects on the collective consciousness of France, Europe and the world.

Llegada Piedras, project for Oracle, Arizona

IMRE MAKOVECZ
HUNGARIAN PAVILION
Expo Seville, Spain

The combination of architecture, music and film has been used here to create a dramatic experience, a message in 20 minutes about Hungarian history, culture and way of life.

The orientation of the Hungarian Pavilion, for the Expo 92, Seville, is north-southerly lengthways, taking 50 x 17.5 metres of the area situated in the neighbourhood of the Austrian and Vatican pavilions. Besides the concrete foundation, the building was purely constructed of glass and wood including its main glued supporting pillars.

On first entering a dim, narrow hall the noise of the world outside can still be heard but while climbing the stairs the sounds of a montage of music and natural noise can be perceived. Six bell towers are spaced along two walls, dividing the area up into two parts diagonally.

'Hungary' is within the Pavilion's two walls – the left-hand side gives a view of the western part of Hungary and the eastern part is on the right-hand side.

Curved stairs lead down to the west part of the area where a huge oak tree with its roots can be seen embedded in a glass-made ceiling. The tree's roots pushed beneath represent Hungarian architecture and folk art, knowledge that is still alive though buried. On walking around the tree, the ground floor gates of the towers open and bells start tolling. These in turn remind all of Europe of the heroic times of the country's history, not only the battles fought against the Turks 500 years ago but the present struggle as well. Beyond the gates a film is being shown about the Hungarian scenery, history and every-day life.

When these pictures have vanished, the face-shaped towers are illuminated revealing the exit.

The Hungarian Pavilion was built by MAKONA Construction Designing and Enterprising Ltd, authorised by the Ministry of International Economic Relations of the Hungarian Republic. This construction can be regarded as the only one of its type since it was carried out by the coordination of private enterprisers and small-holders.

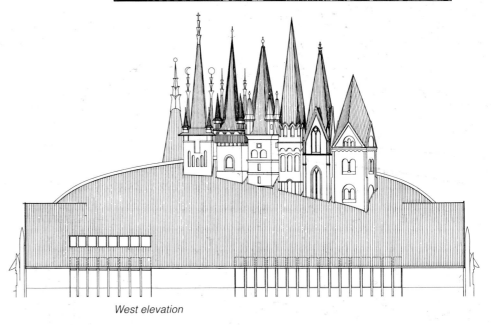

West elevation

FERENC SALAMIN
KUGLICS HOUSE
Budapest, Hungary

Budapest is situated on either side of the river Danube. The Western side, Buda, was built on hills and is wooded with many look-out towers and ski-tracks. In the outskirts rural and suburban built form alternate with nature. On the hillside dwellings lie amongst garden trees.

The Kuglics House is located on a hillside of yellowish stone, soil has been blown away and huge rocks randomly protrude from the ground. Here stand boulders, eroded by the wind and frost, almost like the house itself. The house could have grown from this rock along with the fence and garden.

The building, designed by Salamin of the Axis Architectural Office, MAKONA Group, consists of three storeys and a cellar and was built from 1987-91. The living surface is 230 metres square, the cellar 95 metres square. A fireplace was built in the centre of the sitting room and the terrace has views of the surrounding hills.

LEFT: Elevation; RIGHT: Conceptual sketch

ARBEIDSGRUPPEN
WALDORF SCHOOL
Stavanger, Norway

The school is designed for building in stages; thus necessitating a system of units individually comprehensive and complete. The variation of uniform units depends upon functional consideration and position within the total structure.

Semi-climatised zones were introduced as temperature buffers between outside and inside, creating the need for a continuous structure. All the materials have been chosen with a view to creating a healthy internal environment, not only as regards to light, air and colours.

A wavy roof-scape is another early design motif. The chosen H-P roof structure depicts a character hard to visualise due to its change of two directions at the same time, bearing resemblance to the image of ecological thinking: to be able to see different, independent systems or organisms work together within a totality. The building is erected as a regular system of in-situ concrete columns and floors. The longitudinal spine serves as fire barrier, services zone and corridor.

The roof is carried on primary beams of laminated timber and is covered with slate tiles. Internal walls of spine are of in-situ concrete, rendered masonry and light expanded concrete. External walls of damp-open timber construction, externally timber panelling of varying dimensions, internally plaster/fibre-board.

Insulation material is injected cellulose-fibre. Ceilings are covered with cement/fibre-boards, plasterboard or timber panelling. Floor finishes are linoleum, ceramic tiles and wood. Internal wall finishes are of plaster/ fibre-board, timber panelling and plywood.

The Waldorf School in Stavanger, built 1989-91, possesses a firm rhythm typical of Structuralism, though with a number of deviations and variations and a general appearance close to the expressive character of Rudolf Steiner's model buildings. The result is a free and independent building quite rid of anthroposophical cliches. *Ulf Grønvold*

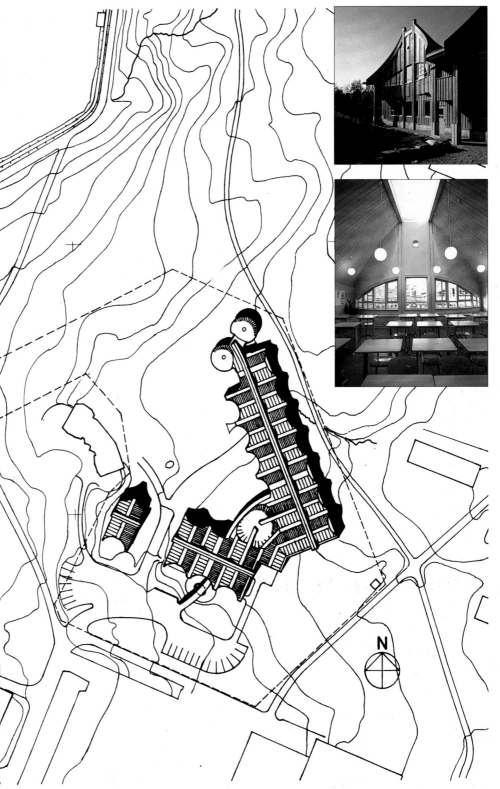

Site plan; OVERLEAF BELOW: East elevation

48

JOHN LAUTNER
HOUSE AT LECHUZA POINT
California

The house is situated on a rocky point of land on the coast to the north-west of Los Angeles. The clients required a non-traditional, part-time beach-front holiday house which became a permanent residence as the project progressed, in 1983.

The house has an arched roof tilted purposely towards the ocean to protect against the setting sun and direct the internal view and space towards the Pacific Ocean. The undulating roof edge, freely cut, flows with the rocks and water edge below and avoids the usual single-aspect picture window. This roof provides a definable enclosure yet gives a free, casual and ungeometric flowing space for living in intimate contact with the ocean. Additional boulders were brought in to further define the space and for use, in conjunction with poured-in-place concrete, as furniture. Much of the furniture and cabinetry is built-in, including a master water bed shell. Concrete and stone flooring complete the beach house environment.

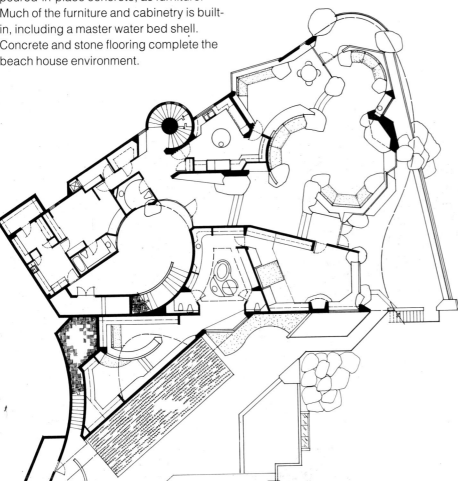

Ground floor plan

DOUG GAROFALO
SUBURBAN CAMOUFLAGE
Chicago

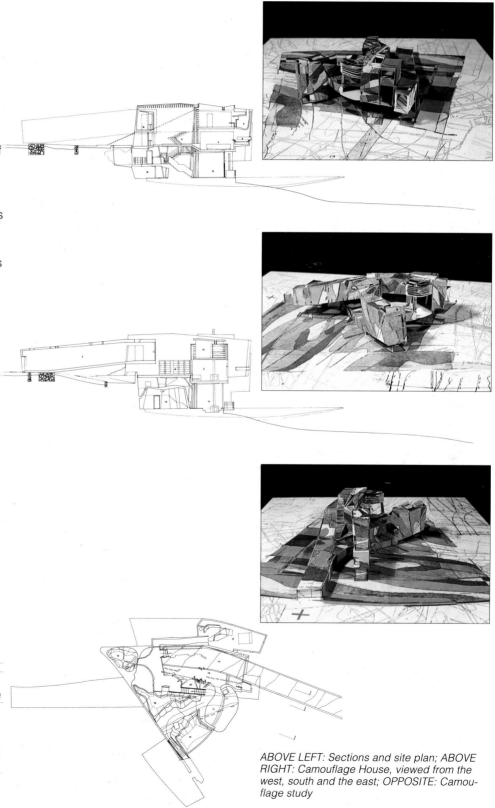

One might approach the suburban dream in a variety of ways: as a cultivated environment of distraction from the rigours of urban or rural scenes; as the outcome of automobile technology coupled with the romance of a house-in-the-country; or perhaps suburbia represents the refinement of an insidious caste system. Each reveals the 'dream' in suburbia as an act of invisibility. The goal of the perfect domestic setting disguises the impracticality of achieving such an end: could architecture *really* replace a dream?

What could be thought of as commodious about a suburban dream house? Its geographical situation has more to do with what automobiles provide; and it is perhaps the suburban interior that needs rearranging. The traditional programme for a house is fabricated on room names suggesting activities or things which symbolise activities. If the room name is freed from its traditional role as the signifier of an event, then rooms themselves might be events. The rooms in the 'oneiric' house would suggest dreams, since the traditional dream house produces a boredom by acquiring the full satisfaction of the wish.

The 'client' in this instance is a corporation developing a suburb 20 miles southwest of Chicago. The proposed development, 'Falling Water', is located on a 104 acre tract of wooded land, and is intended for 121 homes. Falling Water seeks to be a safe haven of shared values balanced with a respect for privacy, complete with state-of-the-art security and a set of architectural covenants to preserve the aesthetic quality of the neighbourhood . . .

The camouflagic response addresses a number of paradoxes: the absurdity of a multi-million dollar home serenely fitting into the 'natural' landscape which is neither natural nor secluded but a manicured piece of theatre; the desire for village tranquillity in a community made possible through speed and telecommunications; and finally, the self-contradictory conclusion that a community of shared values may be sustained through property and taste surveillances.

ABOVE LEFT: Sections and site plan; ABOVE RIGHT: Camouflage House, viewed from the west, south and the east; OPPOSITE: Camouflage study

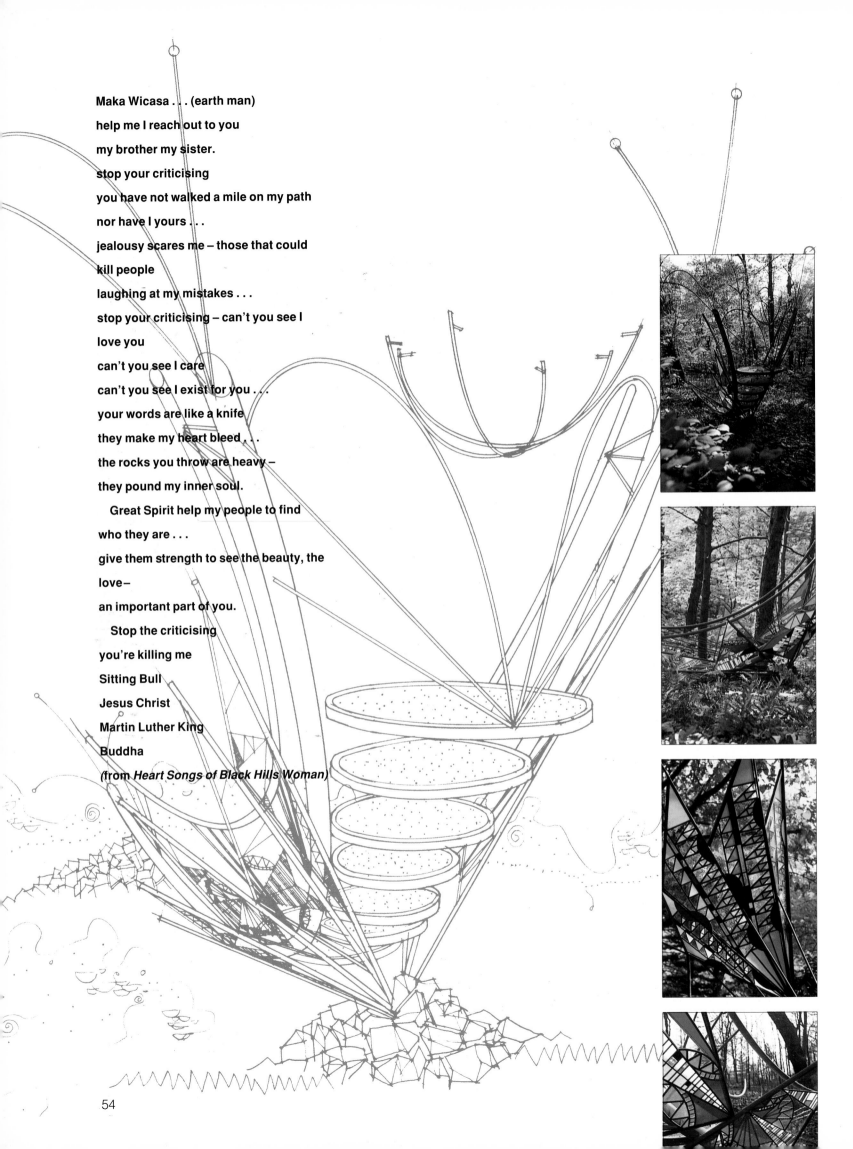

Maka Wicasa . . . (earth man)

help me I reach out to you

my brother my sister.

stop your criticising

you have not walked a mile on my path

nor have I yours . . .

jealousy scares me – those that could

kill people

laughing at my mistakes . . .

stop your criticising – can't you see I

love you

can't you see I care

can't you see I exist for you . . .

your words are like a knife

they make my heart bleed . . .

the rocks you throw are heavy –

they pound my inner soul.

    Great Spirit help my people to find

who they are . . .

give them strength to see the beauty, the

love –

an important part of you.

    Stop the criticising

you're killing me

Sitting Bull

Jesus Christ

Martin Luther King

Buddha

(from *Heart Songs of Black Hills Woman*)

54

TERRY BROWN
MAKA WICASA, STONE RESIDENCE
Cincinnati, Ohio

The brief called for six yard lights and a bird feeder to be designed for the wooded site surrounding the client's home in Hyde Park, Cincinnati. The house, built in the late 70s by the architect Carl Strauss, resides in a rural area with trees and coarse grass, thereby providing an ideal location for Terry Brown's work.

The materials chosen for the project are concrete, slag glass, structural steel and stained glass. This combination fuses strength, sensitivity and texture. It is for this reason that these materials are often a favourite in Brown's work.

The basic construction of the yard lights is a concrete, hollow pyramid, bejewelled by encrusted slag glass. These volcanic forms appear to erupt from the earth, catching the light during the day, and glowing from an internal light during the night. The concrete structure conceals the lighting system and supports the delicate glass designs which spring feather-like from the glassy mound. They form enigmatic shapes, indeed one could interpret them as exotic butterflies or feathered arrows or any number of organism from the animal or plant kingdom. The glass surfaces are both translucent and transparent, forming abstract colour and light.

The bird feeder consists of a sweep of steel arcs which form steps leading to feeding trays. The structure doubles as an observation post with a view of the house and the lighting sculptures. These objects adorn the forested area and connect the inhabitants with the earth, as Terry Brown himself commented:

> . . . to my way of thinking the Stone project is architecture of the highest form . . . it certainly possesses all of the critical aspects of any good work of architecture – a conceptual sense of the joining of material, pragmatics and form . . . a heightened relationship to the earth and a childlike sense of wonder.

These functional, grove-land sculptures take their inspiration from the lyrics of a song by a Lakota Sioux musician.

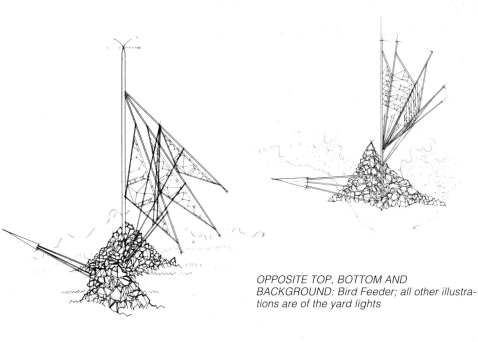

OPPOSITE TOP, BOTTOM AND BACKGROUND: Bird Feeder; all other illustrations are of the yard lights

LESTER KORZILIUS
SYLVAN HILL COUNTRY RESIDENCE
Connecticut

This project is a family residence in north-west Connecticut, approximately two hours from New York City. This house will be a permanent home when completed. The site is private and heavily wooded, and is eight acres in size.

The primary concept is to create a series of pavilions set among a sylvan forest, on a gently sloping site. Nature interacts, and is one of the main design elements of this house. The pavilions are set among trees, some of which pass through portions of the house, creating a sense of living in a forest. Additionally, there are several rock outcrops on the site which are retained and integrated into the design of the house.

Views are to the southeast, in a sweep of approximately 115 degrees. This view is of exceptional beauty down and along a small valley. No man-made structures can be seen from the house. The pavilions take maximum advantage of the natural setting by their siting among the trees and orientation to the sun. Very few trees are removed from this wooded site to accommodate this project. The concave curvature on the view side of the pavilions optimises the available views. The three pavilions are staggered so that the view from any one pavilion is not blocked by another pavilion. The glazing of the pavilions also catches the southern sun, which is an important consideration for buildings in this latitude.

This project is the creation of meaningful places. These places/spaces are gradated from public to private. Inspirational precedents for this concept include Aldo van Eyck's 'Wheels of Heaven' church project and Louis Kahn's Unitarian Church in Rochester, New York. Timo and Tuomo Suomalainen's 'Church in the Rock' in Helsinki was a strong influence with regard the nature of the pavilion spaces. The spaces in this project are gradated as follows: public space; semi-public space, ie the land surrounding the house, and the private access road; controlled transitional space, ie the open, trellis covered entry court; semi-private space, such as the interior entry and gallery space; private space, ie the three pavilions are each containers of the most intimate spaces in the house.

This project will be a retirement home for one couple. This meant that the space and layout of the home had to be spacious enough to allow a couple to be in the home on a nearly full time basis.

The internal heated area of the house is approximately 4600 foot squared. There are approximately a further 1860 foot squared of outdoor decks, garages, greenhouse and basement.

Beginning from the motor court there is a three car garage, greenhouse and trellis covered entry court. The greenhouse is curved along a serpentine cedar wall, and is used as a spatial ordering device in the entry sequence. The first pavilion contains the kitchen and family room that will be used on a daily basis. The second pavilion contains a study and a formal entertainment area that will be used infrequently. The third pavilion contains the master suite, ie, the master bedroom and master bathroom. Connecting the pavilions is a curved gallery. The curved west wall of this gallery is used for the display of the client's excellent art collection. The guest wing has two small bedrooms. A basement is excavated below the guest wing, and contains a wine cellar, storage area and mechanical equipment.

The choice of materials is kept simple. The house is of wood frame construction, with laminated wood beams used for the deck cantilevers and the construction of the roof. Curved laminated beams are used for the perimeter roof ring beams. The decks cantilever from the building by eight feet. This cantilever gives definition to the pavilions and enhances the private nature of the outdoor decks.

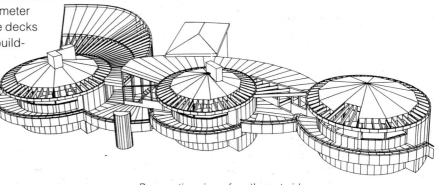

Perspective view of north-east side

57

ARTHUR DYSON
LENCIONI RESIDENCE
Sanger, California

The building programme indicated by the clients was both extensive and specific. Their requirements could be summarised by a compact dwelling that would provide for an informal lifestyle for daily living, offer an intimate atmosphere for small evening gatherings, and serve as a focus for larger outdoor entertainments. Their specific requests included a shop to perform metalwork and various other jobs, and a kitchen arrangement that would be able to look north to the front entry, south to the outdoor living areas, and be surrounded by a breakfast bar for casual family and social dining. The clients also explicitly expressed an affinity for curves and arches without a Spanish or Mediterranean motif, a fondness for shingled exteriors, and a preference for an open plan interior with high ceilings. They were also drawn to A-frame designs but were concerned about the extreme height at the apex of the roof common with plans wide enough to accommodate their needs.

The secluded, wooded site, several hundred yards from its nearest neighbours and screened from public view, afforded the opportunity to explore their desires for a more expressive design than an urban lot with closely adjoining buildings would allow. Being in the 100 year flood plain mandated a finish floor three feet above grade, which presented difficulties in balancing the desired interior height with the flat, open glade in which the house was centred. The resolution occurs through the integration of two structural curves. The upper curve encloses the maximum amount of space with the minimum of materials, while the inverted lower curve provides a visual counterpoint to the arching roof by swinging downwards to the foundation. A berm raised onto the foundation anchors the house in a grassy carpet, setting the whole composition comfortably on the ground. The flowing shape of these dominant curves establishes the sinuous form of the exterior surface finished in red cedar shingles.

The first floor contains living, dining, and kitchen areas as well as a shop and garage. The second floor area is visually connected to the first floor through opened interior walls where possible, enclosing the bedroom, bath, and study loft where privacy is required. Interior finish and other metalwork has been executed by the client, including ornamental stair balusters, chimney cap, shop window frame, and gate at the entrance to the property. Each facet of the design attends some specific desire by the client for a unique and personal expression in architecture, and the residence continues to develop as an articulation of their character.

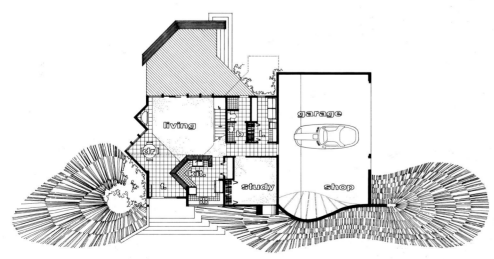

Ground floor plan

JAKSHA RESIDENCE
Madera County, California

Environmental relationships with the site and the need to meet a wide variety of client preferences determined the solution for this three bedroom dwelling. Placed comfortably apart from other houses on a small hill in a rural subdivision of approximately 43 acre parcels, the elevated site has a gently rolling terrain covered with natural grasses that features particularly advantageous views of sunsets and city lights in the distance. Both clients work during the week and enjoy spending their weekends in the yard, thus occupying their home primarily in the evenings. In addition to housing these living patterns, they expressed a keen preference for angular architecture. The factors together with solar considerations determined the orientation of the house and development of the floor plan.

The need to position the house for maximum solar benefit, to enjoy the sunsets, and at the same time to allow for viewing of the city lights introduced contradictory elements in generating the form and axis of the plan. These problems were resolved by focusing on the clients' desire for an angled structure. A minimum of fenestration was utilised on the street (north) elevation to maximise privacy and solar tempering, while large expanses of glazing are opened on the south elevation. The glazing planes face magnetic north (16 degrees west of true north). The building's side walls, which direct the eye, face the city view (22.5 degrees east of magnetic north). The unfoldment of interior spaces and exterior decking between these angles permits a range of external focus according to desire and time of day.

Within the wingspread of the walls, the open plan of the living room, dining room and kitchen is separated only by floor level changes. A continuous skylight for stargazing separates the two major roof planes covering the living room, and an open trellis light deck lowers the scale of the space to separate this space from the dining room while permitting visual access. The use of large overhangs and trellises allows the clients to enjoy the sunset while providing protection from the hot sun.

Choice of building materials was limited due to budget constraints. Cedar 'corral lumber' (1 x 12 inch) was used as exterior siding with diagonally cut two inch square cedar battens covering edge irregularities and allowing for shrinkage. The siding enters the interior at specific places where glass reveals the continuation of interior and exterior planes. Since rolled roofing was used for cost savings, to avoid the exposed tar at horizontal laps these areas were raised and flashed by the use of 2 x 6 inch nailers cut on a diagonal. Inside, a large on-site granite boulder was raised in place and set on a concrete block platform beside the living room steps. Sheet rock walls and ceilings with painted doors and trim provide a crisp tension between the rough sawn cedar siding, exposed aggregate flooring, and natural boulder. The textures of these structural materials and the natural surroundings of the site combine with the compositional interplay of light and horizon to fulfil the character of living space sought by the clients.

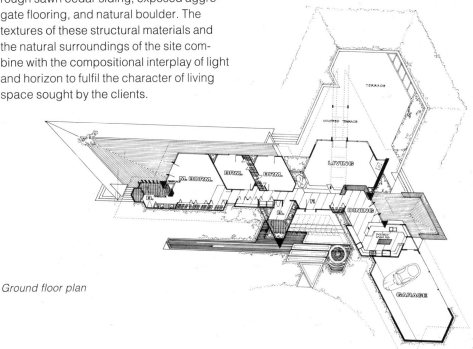

Ground floor plan

SIMPSON RESIDENCE
Fresno, California

The design of this house for a contractor/developer presented an opportunity to prove the economic benefits of creative architectural response. Located in a subdivision designed around a man-made lake, the corner entrance to the site opens from a narrow street frontage on a cul-de-sac into a fan-shaped waterfront lot. Within these irregular boundaries, the contractor asked for a redwood home whose elevations would contrast with the homogeneous surroundings of the subdivision to attract customers.

Site orientation, terraces and decks make this home appear much larger than neighbouring structures of similar size. The design solution emphasises privacy from both the street and adjoining houses while maximising openness for enjoyment of the lake frontage. The front entry penetrates into the inner part of the lot, establishing a sense of depth that belies the narrowness of the street access. This perception is further extended by recognising landscaping effects from adjoining properties.

The entire living focus of the residence is directed towards the south, facing the open reach of the lake, not only to engage aesthetic values and balance site disposition, but for the important economy of solar tempering. The living room terrace steps down towards the lake with a series of inward turning levels that form an outdoor seating area around an open fire-pit. Softer seasonal illumination enters through clerestory windows during winter, while harsher summer sunlight is screened by the angle of the roof. Off the master bedroom, living space also thrusts out towards the lake on a cantilevered second floor deck, whose aproned redwood prow conceals the view of the land and affords privacy while appearing to be upon the open water. The master bedroom shares a fireplace with the master bath providing both with an added sense of luxury. In the bath the ceramic tile hearth

extends itself to form a seating area and also becomes a deck surrounding the tub.

All exterior walls are sheathed in 1 x 8 inch horizontal redwood flush, square edge tongue-and-groove siding with 6 x 6 inch douglas fir trim strips. The closed front gable ends are covered with medium cedar shakes following the angle of the roof pitch. Double entry doors leading into the home are constructed of redwood siding and various sized wood strips designed to carry the lines of the house.

The results of this solution proved to be most beneficial. The design attracted three to four times the number of visitors as the adjoining models. Because of its uniqueness and developed sense of presence, this house sold for a much higher profit than the surrounding homes. The builder recognised the effort and vision of sometimes varying from the norm, which could prove profitable in both added publicity exposure and financial gain.

CENTRE: Detail of banisters; BELOW: Second floor plan; OVERLEAF, FROM L TO R: Conceptual sketch; Ground floor plan

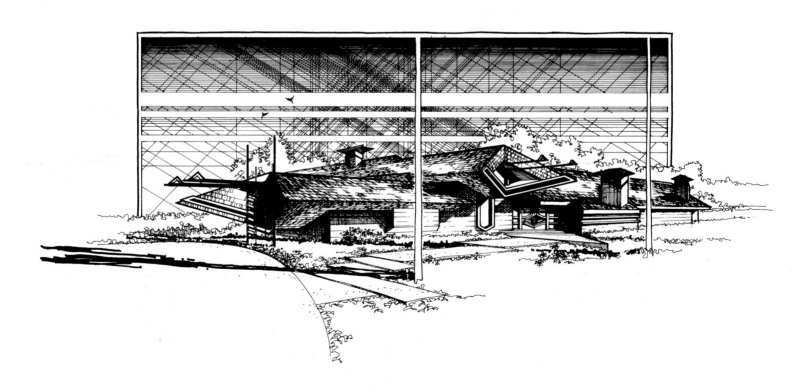

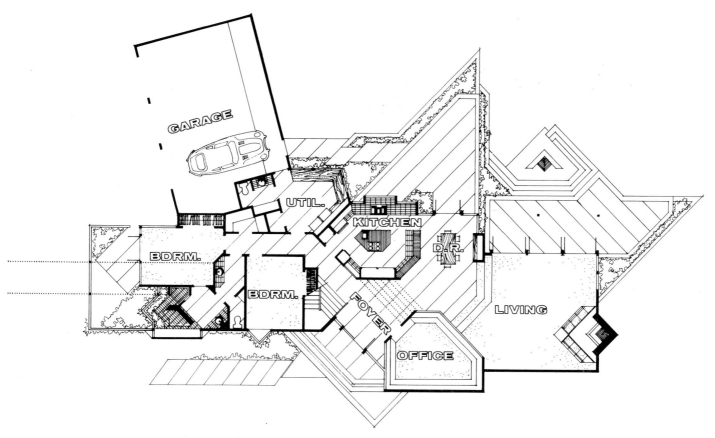

DANIEL LIEBERMANN
ALEXANDER RESIDENCE
Berkeley, California

Built on a steep amphitheatre site containing dispersed 1930s redwood cottages; this 3,500 foot square building makes use of the main cottage which establishes the base of three levels. The 'kiva'-like new structure integrates the new and old, forming the main kitchen and dining area. Rising up from this level is a semi-circular timber stair connecting to the social floor. The social floor runs north and south with the contours perpendicular to the slope, as a series of connected interior terraces. Outside this level is the main outdoor terrace formed also as a connected series of smaller terraces. From here an impressive view of the Golden Gate Bridge as well as the bay is opened up. As a partial mezzanine to the social floor, the level above is the bedroom level. From all levels running north and south are terraces, decks, pools and balconies.

Here, as in other Liebermann structures, the plan morphology is a direct and strict function of the natural undulating and concave steep geomorphology. The terraced and curvilinear plan-form and section is based on maximum site and structural efficiency, least site disturbance and least constructional redundancy. The topo-logarithmic curvature elicits a radio-centric framing structure resting on central columns. This building is an example of a highly integrated sub- and super-structure. This is exemplified by the structurally continuous shell walls embedded into grade and their grade-beams 'trussed' connectors as well as the deep bedrock piers supporting steel moment-arm columns at the glass 'heat-mirror' walls supporting the built-up timber roof. The building was completed in 1989.

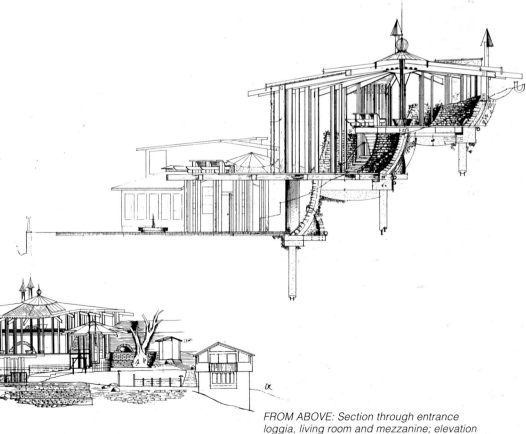

FROM ABOVE: Section through entrance loggia, living room and mezzanine; elevation

LIEBERMANN AND PAINE RESIDENCE
Pine II, Mill Valley, California

The building plan is an oblate partial ellipse, a function of topography. Morphic harmony of cut and fill, bench, slab, and wall to land is a basic applied principle. The slab is perched on its bench with a keel-like longitudinal rib unifying and keying the whole into bedrock. Congruent with that harmony is a liberal flowing roof cover. Carrying the whole roof is a skeletal radial hyperboloid column of pipe, bar and board, cantilevered from a caisson integrated with the slab. The roof is free to flex with the column under expected severe seismic shock. A continuous concave elliptical wall, curved in plan, section and elevation has been cut into the slope forming the multi-levelled terrace that is the plan. In this masonry retaining wall, sleeving the frame, are steel fork stanchions which rise up supporting the roof, ultimately forming a continuous camber at the circumferential edge of the roof. Out of this formed concavity and the limits of existing local technology, Liebermann has aimed at freeing space and movement, creating a free plan of structural lightness and arboreal ambience.

The floor plan comprises a one room dwelling of about 1,000 foot square. Areas are differentiated by change of grade, roof height, folding 'door-walls' and opaque translucent partitions. The roof and *raum* can be felt from the central living area from which the whole is suggested. The apex and origin of the radiality, the central column, holds the highest glazing and view, opening up a wall of glass. This wall with the great pine tree and forest just outside contribute to the plastic spatiality and linear climax of the living area that is the column. The big wall and the land dam, with the fireplace and stack, express the layered concentricity of slab, edge, arch, wall and roof frame. Due to a careful welding of maxima and minima, high and low, long and short, heavy and light, and open and closed, relatively great freedom of movement and sense of expansiveness is achieved. A high operative efficiency in minimal area. The residence was completed in 1965.

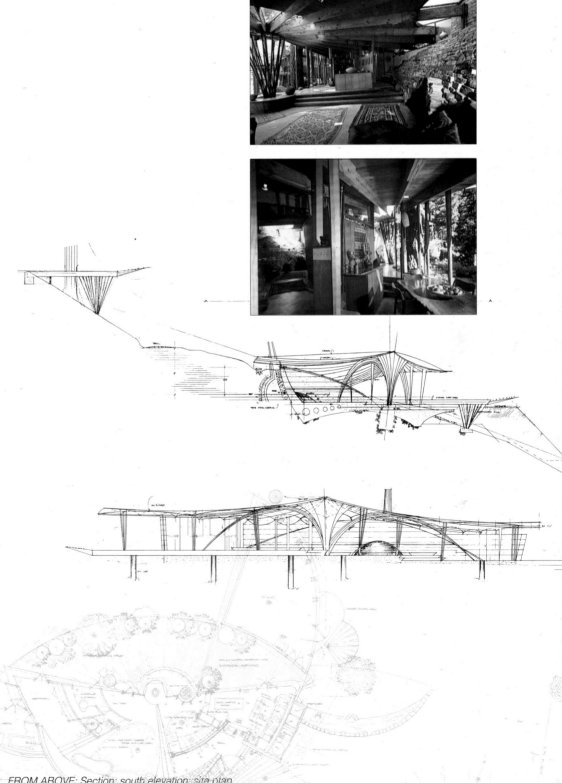

FROM ABOVE: Section; south elevation; site plan

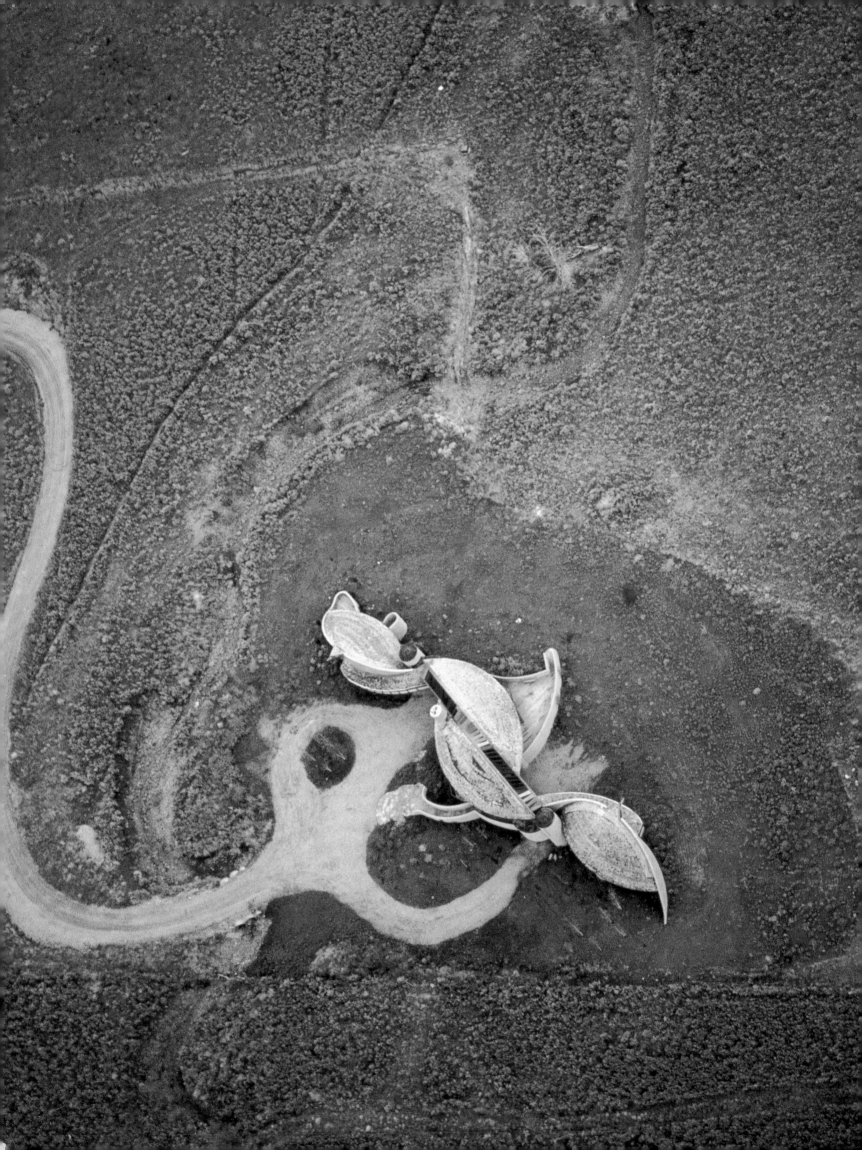

BART PRINCE
WHITING RESIDENCE
Albuquerque, New Mexico

Henry Whiting, the owner of a Frank Lloyd Wright house in Bliss, Idaho was interested in building a vacation house in the Sun Valley area which he could later sell. Thus, the programme was geared towards designing an interesting and functional house that would be more than the usual 'spec' type building but which would appeal to a wide variety of people who like to spend a part of the year in Sun Valley. The site is a beautiful 12 acre tract situated in a valley between the soft rolling mountains and hills of the area. The client was interested in a design which would pick up the 'feel' of the surrounding landscape rather than mimicking the so-called 'regional' log and wood buildings of the area.

The house stretches out over the landscape rather than being centred in a confined structure. This allowed for the separation of the master suite at one end and the guest rooms at the other. Each has its own spectacular views of the valley and mountains in the distance without seeing any of the rest of the house. The main living area is the central portion of the design and is raised above the site over the garages below. A ramp leads from the outside up to the low-ceilinged enclosed entry from which a turn is made to the left, opening to the high skylit space of the living room. The two serpentine masonry walls extend from this large space in either direction to enclose the bedrooms at each end of the house. The curving roofs are created by intersecting laminated beams, one lying horizontally and the other rising vertically. These are connected by straight beams and covered with ship-lap decking which is exposed as the ceilings. The central volume consists of two of these partial spheres which are slid apart along the axis of the skylight which separates them. The stone path below this skylight emphasises the axis and the separation of the more formal from the less formal portions of this main space.

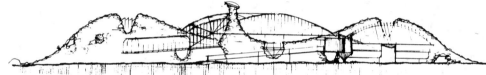

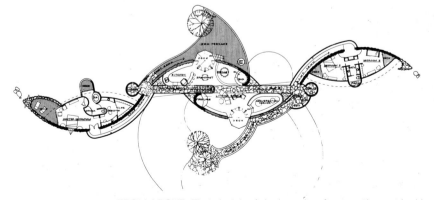

FROM ABOVE: First sketch of design, view from north-west looking south-east; main level floor plan

PRINCE RESIDENCE
Albuquerque, New Mexico

This house was designed for a rocky, one acre parcel of land at the base of the Sandia Mountain range at the north-eastern edge of Albuquerque, New Mexico. The views to the west extend for 100 miles or more over the Rio Grande Valley to the distant mountains. The owners were interested in a design which would open to the distant views as well as the views to the large mountains to the east. The house is designed for entertaining; thus the living area contains the kitchen, dining room, family room, and living room all on several levels in one large space. Above this large space is a series of segmented steel tube-beams which radiate from the kitchen side out towards the view side of the large space. Suspended from these are three large disks of radial laminated beams with tongue-and-groove decking between them forming the ceiling and roofs of the area.

The large garages are set beneath the guest bedroom wing completely out of view. The curving masonry wall along the north side of the house forms a shield to the winter winds and provides privacy for the guest bedrooms at ground level.

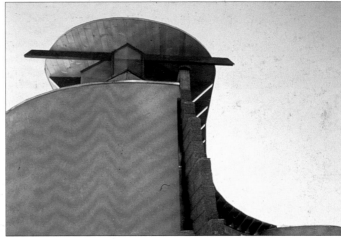

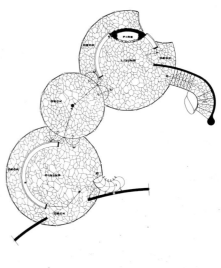

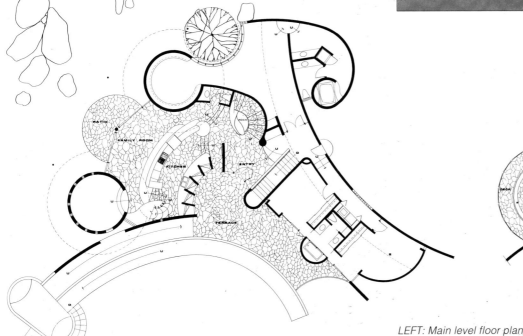

LEFT: Main level floor plan; RIGHT: Upper level floor plan

73

MICKEY MUENNIG
FOULKE RESIDENCE
Big Sur, California

This house, designed for two inhabitants, is sited above the ruins of a locally historic water wheel grinding mill. The structure's imagery reflects the music of the river passing over the mill's partially remaining foundations, the spirit of the rolling water wheel, the owner's Germanic origins and infinity of the steeply sloped single roofs of Northern Europe, a visible triple arched bridge crossing the river, and the highly contoured surrounding landscape.

The structure consists of 18 foot long 2 x 6 foot boards cut from local pine trees. Nails resist shear between each member, and a threaded steel rod compresses the 2 x 6 foot boards along the ridge, forming a wooden shell structure.

POST RANCH INN
Big Sur, California

This guest inn, 30 room, reception, restaurant, is designed to give people a sense of nature during their stay. It has earth sheltered rooms, designed to recess into the earth along the ocean side of the property, allowing views over them. On the east side of a narrow ridge, it has tree houses, with poles on concrete piers to overlook the earth sheltered rooms and protect the tree roots. It has cylindrical rooms stacked on top of each other in order to capture beautiful views of the ocean. It has a six room butterfly building for conventions.

The restaurant is approached through a tunnel underground and opens into a magnificent view of the ocean.

The reception lodge, placed off the ridge top, contains a gift shop. Parking is restricted so that no cars are allowed on the hill.

FROM ABOVE: Upper Floor Plan of a Unit B 'Tree House'; Exterior and interior views of a 'Tree House'; Sketch of a 'Tree House'; OPPOSITE: Passive Solar Greenhouse Studio, Big Sur

WILL MILLER
MILLER RESIDENCE
New Smyrna Beach, Florida

The design concept was to create shelter, respect the site and to elevate the human spirit within an order of poetic depth. Development sections were left uncomposed, only setting down patterns of the original order, thus allowing improvisational artistic development during the building process, which was completed in 1987. This is of immense significance to the architect, as he writes:

There is a constant of seemingly random order that exists in all of Nature. This is not a simple order which is so rigid that all lines must be in strict accordance to a predetermined geometric shape . . . The random order of nature shapes the patterns of rivers, branches of trees, waves in the ocean, wild flowers on a hillside, and veins in our bodies . . . all things in the Universe.

I believe that this same order should exist in the principles which evolve from man's design process . . . whether that be in architecture, music, or any of the arts.

The house is located on a large site of natural vegetated land fronting a tidal estuary of the Intracoastal Waterway. The design is the result of sun angles, tree limbs, views of the estuary, and an orderly, individual expression using natural materials.

The free form was introduced into the rigid 60 degree geometry to allow design expression and to create a third element (to the curve and rigid), that being the element of contrast. The house was to be harmonious with the character of the site, yet contain a study of contrasts . . . solids with voids, angle with curve, textured with smooth.

The house contains around 3,000 foot square of living area on six levels. The dominant interior element is the central gallery which contains stairways to all levels, with a large skylight above. Planters, Soleri bells and mobiles are incorporated as an extension of the design order. Except for the exposed, sandblasted concrete and natural concrete block, all structural and finish materials are various textures of wood.

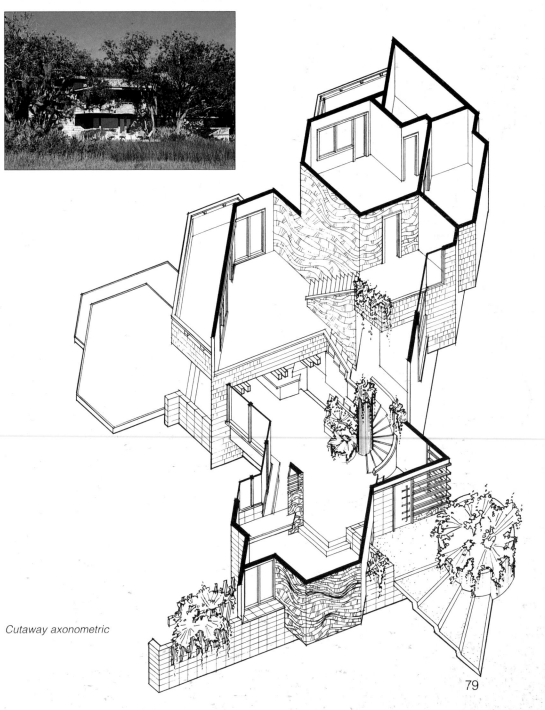

Cutaway axonometric

79

RUEDLINGER RESIDENCE
New Smyrna Beach, Florida

The Ruedlinger Residence is a 7,000 foot square private residence located on three lots at the end of a cul-de-sac along on the edge of the Intracoastal Waterway. The design incorporates wood, glass, stone and, at one of the owner's requests, an 'aeroplane room' on a third storey to allow a panoramic view of the river. Indeed it was very important for Will Miller to accommodate his clients wishes, as he explains:

I am very deliberate and sincere in my belief that the architect should have a deep respect not only for the site, but for the client and their desires as well. The site determines the frame of reference for the design, but it is the client who gives the design purpose. It is then the opportunities and constraints that are established by the client, and inherent in the site, that defines the nature of the order of the design and the potential for greatness that the design contains. The successful result of a sensitive assimilating process I refer to as a design of poetic depth. But, the architect is the one who must provide the poetry and the depth to create the architecture . . . otherwise we have only building. And building is only physical . . . Architecture can contort your mind.

The addition of a swimming pool and an outdoor entertainment area was completed in 1989. A two bedroom guest apartment was added over the detached garage area in 1991.

concept study

HARVEY FERRERO
THE GREAT MIDWEST AGRICULTURE STRUCTURE

The idea of an authentic American Architecture has always been very important to Harvey Ferrero. This is verified by this project which is inspired in form by the towers carrying power across the Midwest countryside. The scheme consolidates the bulk of agricultural concerns into single structures that could be spaced across the landscape much as the power towers. Each structure would have similar requirements but would be individually formed by its specific location, programme and relation to its adjacent structures. A community could live and work on each structure, thus freeing more of the earth for farming. The weather, although not controlled, would be managed to create a favourable environment for efficient agricultural production. The structure would be a constantly moving shifting organism responding to changes in climate. Each structure would also contain a complete village including community buildings and multi-tiered parks. The forms in this project were determined more by intuition and the premise that architecture should include humour. Ferrero expressed his dynamic approach to architecture in a letter to a friend:

When Bruce Goff shot out of the 40s and 50s utilising 'as found' and 'off the shelf' materials to form unique structures that were more in tune with the Cadillac tail fins and the futuristic bent of the times than they seem to be when created; I felt *that* was real American architecture! Unabashed, bold, spatially exciting, naive, exuberantly beautiful . . .

A study of transparency, translucency, layering, movement and the evolving of nature into built forms in an organic way. The work illustrates an architecture consisting of ideas, technologies and materials used in virtually every field today, with the exception of building construction. It depicts a structure which would have the ability to adjust itself externally to changes in nature and internally to programmatic changes. As Ferrero observed:

We are still building as we were 100 years ago. I drool when I see the technology and materials used for more sinister ends in the Gulf War, or applied to winning the America Cup in yachting. That's what we should be working with in architecture; buildings which are constructed of new light materials that can move, change and react to our ever-changing environment. All this plus structures that are beautiful and respond to the American ideal (which is tied up with individualism and a feeling for a vast and different sense of space) that we hopefully still have . . .

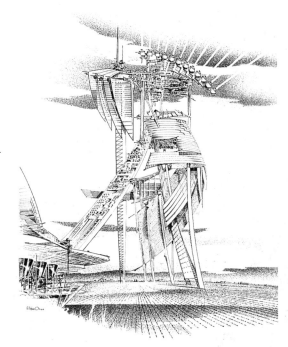

FROM ABOVE: Conceptual sketches – the Great Midwest Agriculture Structure; High-speed Motor Terminal for a town on the North American Plains; OPPOSITE: Composition with architectural implications

EDWARD M JONES
HALAS RESIDENCE
Paradise Valley, Arizona

This residence required a particular internal layout in order to accommodate the needs of the client who is a married, practising psychologist and businessman with grown children. In-house office facilities with provision for patient visitors were required. The solution was a split plan allowing for the doctor's office entry without disturbance to the main residence.

Furthermore conventional rooms were unnecessary; however, the house had to respond to seasonal visits by family members. Interior pocket walls, which disappear to provide a large continuous space or slide into place, have been used to provide flexibility in creating individual sleeping areas for family visits.

A screened porch, with a 'murphy bed', extends the living area to an outdoor sunken patio. Retaining walls peel away from the house to create other outdoor spaces; glazing details are skilfully used to visually integrate exterior views with interior spaces.

A swimming pool provides the family with a primary form of exercise, and emphasises the horizontal nature of this particular mountain site. It also provides a secondary focal axis along the main entry approach.

The design, in accordance with the clients' wishes, put great emphasis on cooking and entertainment facilities. All kitchen cabinetry is custom designed and arranged for specific circulation patterns; its central location services all of the 'public' spaces, yet exterior views are not sacrificed.

The curvilinear geometry directs mountain rain off, and away, from the structure; and the retaining wall form inherently resists lateral earth loads. This ensures that the architectural forms respond to hillside site.

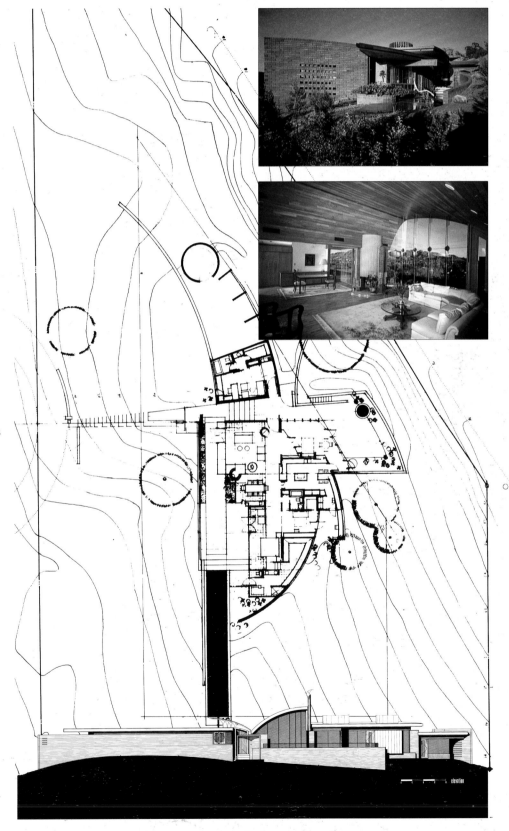

Site plan and elevation

NARI GANDHI
MOON DUST RESIDENCE
Bombay, India

This project, named 'Moon Dust', is one of Nari Gandhi earliest works, a restoration. The original concrete structure has been almost entirely removed, and has been replaced by self-supporting dry-stone arches. Outside, the house is almost entirely hidden by the tropical vegetation, that has been planted there under the direction of the architect, who has a great passion for gardening, during the renovation works.

Nari Gandhi was born in Surat, India, in 1934. After his studies, he spent a long period of time in the United States where he worked with Frank Lloyd Wright. After his return to India in 1964 he did not practice his profession for many years.

Gandhi has a somewhat Spartan lifestyle. He has no formal office and does not produce any drawings for the production of his architecture, preferring to direct his builders personally on site. In this way he bears little resemblance to the traditional figure of the 'professional' architect.

He has a passion for finishes and materials, that he uses with great sensitivity, taking advantage of a patrimony of tradition in Indian craftsmanship.

The conception of each building, (until now he has built only private houses) is deeply bound to its location, that is sometimes chosen by the architect himself. He privileges the sculptural aspect of his buildings, but conceptually they are influenced by his particular social and religious beliefs.

JAMES T HUBBELL
SEA RANCH CHAPEL
California

The Sea Ranch chapel, commissioned by Betty and Robert Buffum, took nearly a year to complete. This non-denominational chapel is dedicated to the memory of Kirk Ditzler whose drawings were the foundation for the design. The roof gives a sense of sweeping, lifting movement, achieved by its manifold profiles. Its structure is inspired by winged forms, yet can be read in a number of different ways. Yet despite the great variety of shape and form, the 360 foot square chapel, achieves an underlying feeling of unity.

James Hubbell has an almost democratic approach to his work. He involves his co-workers according to their abilities; and in this particular project the work was delegated to Tambe Kumaran. He and a team of highly skilled craftsmen set about realising Hubbell's design from a small model and $\frac{1}{4}$ inch engineering drawings.

The chapel sits on a gently sloping site and is constructed on a six inch concrete slab with 12 inch foundation walls, filled with concrete block. The main structure of the building is made of wood siding which was dried and moulded in place to create a shell. The curves of the roof were extremely difficult to accomplish, and Kumaran drew from his boat building experience to achieve both the curves and the chapel's even shingled surface. The materials used for this project are among the architect's favourite: a combination of stained glass, ceramics, metal and plasterwork.

Brightly coloured stained glass windows illuminate the interior which is large enough to seat up to 40 people. The interior is adorned by a white plaster 'flower' sculpture which caps the inner space, lining the ceiling and supporting a metal lighting fixture. A redwood pillar and other free form structures, such as a metal and glass screen in the corner, decorate the inside of Sea Ranch Chapel.

Conceptual sketch

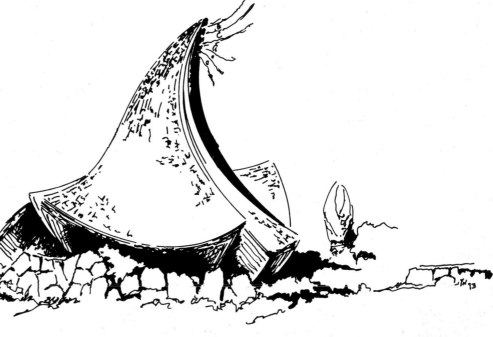

GAY RESIDENCE
San Bernardino Mountains

Built in the San Bernardino Mountains at an altitude of 4,300 feet this family residence has taken ten years to build. Inspired by the spectacular rock formations of the surrounding area it was intended as a retreat into nature, echoing the decomposed, rust-coloured granite. Indeed, James Hubbell's sculptural training is evident in this building.

Although the area generally enjoys a temperate climate it can experience strong winds from the east, thick fog from the coast, thunderstorms and droughts. Covering an area of around 1,800 foot square, the main house and guest room, had to take into consideration these practical concerns. It has been set into side of south-facing hill to shelter from the easterly winds. Furthermore the outdoor patio is protected by a curving stone wall. An extended drought would cause the surrounding woodland to become dry, necessitating a fire-resistant exterior to the building.

The house consists of a main living area with the kitchen, library, solarium, and storage area attached. A guest room is connected by an arcade. The upper floor contains a bedroom, bathroom, balcony and a further guest room.

The architect's working technique is to initially produce quick sketches and clay models which are then used to communicate his ideas with the structural engineer. Flexibility in construction is of paramount importance in a structure of this kind. Therefore black pipe was used for structural elements as it is easy to bend, as are curved I-beams or trusses which were used

for supports. This element of experimentation during the early construction of the house is evident in the guest room, where ceiling heights and curves of walls were altered and refined. This now has a flat tiled roof, surrounded by a railing enabling it to be used as a deck. Family involvement was another aspect to the realisation of 'Rainbow Hill', the Gay Residence. Phil Gay studied building sciences which enabled him to generate the energy calculations for the house. His son Johnathan to a course in residential plumbing and electrical systems.

Craftsmen working at the architect's studio in San Diego produced the plaster, glass and ceramic details which were evolved along with the form of the house and then worked into the finished building. Originally intended to be salmon in colour, the building's stone veneer and stucco coat is in fact painted with red, ochre and umber pigments, inspired by the colours of New Mexico.

Conceptual sketch

HUBBELL RESIDENCE
San Diego, California

The architect and his wife began building their handmade home in 1958, in the mountains of southern California. It was designed in stages, starting with the rectangular office, where the family lived in the early 1960s. The living area was the next stage of building, and this has been made of stone and wood. A stone bench has been built near to an oval fireplace which is set into the wall, as is a mosaic kitchen sink. The room is lit by an elaborate stained-glass window which is skilfully placed in order to frame a view of the town. The master bedroom is reached via a tiled courtyard, which is adorned with a mosaic fountain, and overlooks the tranquil garden. The cavernous bedroom is irregular in form, moulded into hollows with mosaic work decorating the ceiling.

The stained-glass studio, connected to the living space, is the fourth largest building. Yet despite its cathedral-like, lofty, ribbed structure, the studio maintains a human scale. Both the boys' house and bathroom are imaginatively decorated with a whole spectrum of colour; mosaic tiles and stained glass are combined to create truly 'sensational' environments. In his book *From the Earth Up: The Art and Vision of James Hubbell*, Otto Rigan wrote:

> Many of us have moved to the country, getting ourselves 'back to nature', but we have retained our urban mentality. The Hubbell home is free of all such cant from past or present. The functioning parts of the home and studio are divided into six separate structures, inviting the family to experience the shadows, colours, smells and textures of nature while they move from kitchen to bedroom, from studio to storage. The nature that is experienced is not the landscaped and manicured kind but the original indigenous habitat. The hill on which the home is built has been complemented, not changed; revered, not devastated. If the earth's rhythm could be measured with line and volume, these buildings would be a coda, a mere signature of man on the finished whole.

Site plan